HIJACKED

HIJACKED

**A True Story
of Surviving 331 Days
with Somali Pirates**

PRALAV DHYANI

**HARPER
NON-FICTION**

First published in India by Harper Non-Fiction 2025
An imprint of HarperCollins *Publishers* India
HarperCollins *Publishers* India, Cyber City, Building 10-A,
Gurugram, Haryana-122002, India
www.harpercollins.co.in

2 4 6 8 10 9 7 5 3 1

Copyright © Pralav Dhyani 2025

P-ISBN: 978-93-6569-932-6
E-ISBN: 978-93-6569-166-5

The views and opinions expressed in this book are the author's own and the facts are as reported by him, and the publishers are not in any way liable for the same.

Some names and identifying details have been changed to protect the privacy of individuals.

This book contains explicit language and literary depictions of graphic scenes, which some readers may find disturbing. Reader discretion is advised, especially for younger audiences.

Pralav Dhyani asserts the moral right
to be identified as the author of this work.

All rights reserved. No part of this publication may be reproduced, stored in a retrieval system, or transmitted, in any form or by any means, electronic, mechanical, photocopying, recording or otherwise, without the prior permission of the publishers.

Without limiting the exclusive rights of any author, contributor or the publisher of this publication, any unauthorized use of this publication to train generative artificial intelligence (AI) technologies is expressly prohibited. HarperCollins also exercise their rights under Article 4(3) of the Digital Single Market Directive 2019/790 and expressly reserve this publication from the text and data-mining exception.

Typeset in 11.5/15 Adobe Garamond Pro
by HarperCollins *Publishers* India Pvt. Ltd

Printed and bound at
Replika Press Pvt. Ltd.

This book is produced from independently certified FSC® paper
to ensure responsible forest management.

*

HarperCollins *Publishers*, Macken House, 39/40 Mayor Street Upper, Dublin 1,
D01 C9W8, Ireland

To

Mom, Dad and my brother. Thank you for your unwavering encouragement and for standing by me through every decision, no matter how difficult. You three have been my teachers in unique ways, shaping my journey and making it all the more successful

Contents

Important Characters in the Story		ix
Introduction		xi
1.	The Brat That I Was	1
2.	Life at Sea	10
3.	The Hijacking	23
4.	Settling with the Pirates	42
5.	One Hundred Days	66
6.	Maa and Baba	79
7.	The Pirate Code	94
8.	Our New Neighbours	108
9.	Lurking Danger	118

10.	Prepare to Go Hunting	131
11.	Whims and Fancies of Our Captors	151
12.	Bloody T-Shirt	164
13.	'Save Ship, Save Lives'	172
14.	Camaraderie and Brotherhood	179
15.	Burial at Sea	191
16.	A Step Closer to Freedom	198
17.	Uncertainty Lingers	205
18.	Resilience and Recovery	214
	Epilogue	223
	Acknowledgements	229

Important Characters in the Story

RAK Afrikana *Officers and Crew*

1. Rameshwar Naithani, Captain
2. Ali Baig, Chief Officer
3. Zulfikar Shareef aka 'Bada Sahab', Chief Engineer
4. Parjeet Singh Sodhi, Second Officer
5. Mir Balach, Second Engineer
6. Kuldeep Singh, Third Officer
7. Ahmed Durrani, Third Engineer
8. Akbar Khan aka 'Batti Sahab', Electrician
9. Baraka Abdullah, Bosun
10. Abdallah Saidi, Able Seaman
11. Aziz Makame aka 'Uncle', Able Seaman
12. Lucas Manaen aka 'Luca Baba', Welder
13. Abdul Mbarawa, Oiler
14. Hassan Idris, Oiler
15. Muhammed Ali, Chief Cook
16. Rashid Saidi, Steward

Cadets on the RAK Afrikana

1. Zaheer Khan, Senior Cadet
2. Sandeep Singh, Senior Cadet
3. David John, Senior Cadet
4. Samit Choudhary, Senior Cadet
5. Krishna Nair, Senior Cadet
6. Pralav Dhyani, Cadet
7. Shikhar Negi 'SK', Cadet, author's batchmate
8. Anubhav Aarya 'Bade', Cadet, author's batchmate

Somali Pirates

1. Tarjuman, Translator
2. Ahmed, Boss
3. Abdi, Pirate Team Boss
4. Hassan, Pirate Boat Captain
5. Abdullahi, 'Cookie'
6. Mohammed, Storekeeper
7. Omar
8. Jafar
9. Aaden, 'Camel Face'
10. Hamood, 'Cadet Pirate'
11. Abshir, Monkey Island Pirate

Others

1. Author's mother
2. Author's father
3. Pramit, author's elder brother
4. Author's uncle (Mama), author's mother's brother
5. Capt. Vinay Aarya, owner of the *RAK Afrikana*
6. Jogi, a friend in Canada
7. Capt. Nair, Training Superintendent

Introduction

I embarked on my first voyage aboard a merchant ship at age twenty as a deck cadet. This is a rank given to trainees who, once they clear their pre-sea exams, go on to become engineering officers or deck officers.

As I approached the ship, called the *RAK Afrikana*, the first thing I could see from far away was 'SAFETY FIRST' stencilled in big, bold, red letters. By the end of this story, you will realize the importance of these words.

When one is a sailor, there's no avoiding safety drills—there are a lot of them. But doing the same drills again and again, whether on a weekly, monthly or quarterly basis, makes one switch off mentally. At age twenty, as I was, one always seems to have the attitude of '*kuchh nahin hota* (none of this matters)'. So, one ends up going through the drills without really registering anything for practical use.

In 2010, piracy in the Horn of Africa region was at an all-time high. There were almost monthly reports of pirate attacks around the eastern coast of the continent. I was also aware that we were going to cross the territorial waters of Somalia—at the time, the riskiest part of the world's seas. And yet, my brain thought these things could never happen to me.

The idea was to complete my sea service as a cadet and appear for my deck navigation officer exams. I was more excited for my sea service than shore-based theory lectures, because I always enjoyed practical learning more than mugging up notes.

The first whiff of danger came when I was least expecting it. I was having tea with Muhammed Ali, the Chief Cook of the *RAK Afrikana*. He was from Zanzibar, a small island off the Tanzanian coast. He was about five-foot-ten or eleven, and despite being hunchbacked, was a big man, though not very muscular. He must have been fit in his youth, but now, in his mid-fifties, he had a bit of a belly. He had the sort of short-cropped hair very common among Africans, and usually wore white T-shirts, three-quarter-length trousers and safety or sports shoes.

Aboard a ship, sailors are addressed by their ranks instead of their names, and all of us called him 'Chief', or whenever we wanted something extra for our meals, 'Chef'. When I boarded the ship, he was the first person I befriended, because I knew he'd be the man who could get me an extra egg when I wanted one, or help satisfy a food craving at an odd hour. So, I made sure I was there to assist whenever he needed any help handling supplies or support during a port call when we received provisions (ship's rations).

I used to have my morning tea with Muhammed almost every day at the aft deck—he would have a big cup of black tea, while mine would be milky. We would talk about life in Zanzibar, in India, and the places we had both been to. I tried to learn what I could from his decades of experience at sea, as any cadet tries to. After all, regardless of whether one is a cadet or a captain, the more you ask, the more you learn. Discussions with others about seamanship always come in handy.

When you have as much experience of sailing as Muhammed Ali did, you can spot something unusual from miles away. A slight change in the wind, and their sixth sense gets alerted. One day as we were having our tea, he stopped talking to me mid-sentence and began looking at something behind me. He spoke in his native Swahili to the ship's steward, Rashid, who ran to fetch binoculars.

'What happened? Why are you panicking?' I asked, confused.

'I think I see a boat in the water,' Muhammed replied.

That didn't sound concerning to me. We were at sea, so obviously there would be boats out there, or cargo carrying ships like ours. So I asked him why he suddenly seemed so stressed.

'Pirates, *baana*,' he said, using the Swahili word for 'sir', which has evolved to be used informally among friends.

My heart leapt into my mouth. Till that moment, pirates had been an abstract concept in my head, people I was sure I would never get to see for real.

Ours was an unarmed ship. In fact, at the time, the idea of having armed guards on board merchant ships was being hotly debated in shipping circles. Some believed that even crew members should be trained to use weapons, but there were not many takers for that. Some ships had started taking precautionary measures by installing razor wires on the deck and keeping high-pressure water hosepipes in a standby position. But the *RAK Afrikana* didn't have either of those. Even if we did, this would only delay the pirates. If they came with guns, the only option would be to try and outrun them before they climbed aboard.

Lucky for us, the thing Muhammed had seen turned out to be just a drum floating in the open waters. I could barely see it, even with the binoculars.

'How the fuck did you even pick it up with your naked eye?' I asked in wonder.

Muhammed replied that even though he was a cook, if someone put him at the helm of the ship, he could take us through this sea route with his eyes closed, at least till Zanzibar.

This false alarm really woke me up, and I started taking my safety drills a lot more seriously. The threat of piracy had just become real in my mind, and I truly needed to understand what was to be done if they ever attacked our ship.

A few months after this incident, my worst fears did come true.

We had just finished our cargo operations in the beautiful island country of Seychelles and were heading to Zanzibar, where my senior cadets were about to sign off and go back home, and new cadets were about to sign on. This would make me and my two batchmates, Shikhar (whom we called 'SK') and Anubhav ('Bade'), senior cadets. I also had a nickname, 'Bonge', but more on that later.

We were excited, because being a senior cadet comes with its own perks—think of it like being a final-year student in college. But what we got instead was a situation in which the entire crew of the ship was consigned to the position of junior cadets.

Our main engine chose the worst possible part of the ocean to break down, right off the coast of Seychelles, and soon, three or four gun-toting Somali pirates took over our ship. They made us steer it to within a few nautical miles from the coast of Somalia, where we were ordered to drop anchor.

In captivity, one spends a lot of time thinking about death. There was fear of having a gun pointed at me, with the threat of the trigger being pulled at any moment. There was still hope that I wouldn't get to experience the feeling. But I did experience it—two months after the hijacking.

I stood on the deck, my hands in the air, as one of the pirates pointed an AK-47 right at my forehead, the tip of the barrel barely an inch from my skin. My heart was beating faster than ever; I was shitting bricks as I waited for my brains to leak out of the imminent gunshot wound.

In the movies, when someone is about to die, their life flashes in front of their eyes. But when the gun was an inch from my forehead, my mind went blank, waiting for the pirate's next move. My life depended on that one-dollar bullet in his gun. How do I know the price? Because after I returned from captivity, I worked for a company providing maritime security guards to ships navigating the waters that I had been unable to cross safely. A one-dollar bullet was all that was needed to end everything for a person and their family.

I looked at the pirate holding the gun. This one always reeked of something other than just tobacco, which meant that we could always smell him before we saw him. The tops of his cigarette packs were always torn, presumably to make roaches. He was a six-foot-tall, skinny, bald, older man with a white goatee, always dressed in shorts or three-quarters, and usually with a bed sheet wrapped around him like a shawl. His teeth were yellow, and one of them was chipped. Even his eyes were yellow, as if he had jaundice. He had an elongated, V-shaped face with a pronounced jawline, because of which we had nicknamed him 'Jafar', after the villain in Disney's *Aladdin*. He tried hard to be intimidating, though he didn't need to, because he had the gun in his hands.

Jafar had been around from the time we had anchored in Somali waters, but we hadn't interacted with him much, compared to the other pirates. He and the others were always eating 'khat', a plant that looked indistinguishable from any other. We wondered why human beings would eat jungle grass like that, and each of us had our own theories about why they loved it so much. Someone said it was good for their sex life and libido, but then we wondered why they were having it on the ship, miles away from their partners. The logical reason was that it gave them a high.

Much later, I found out that khat is indeed a stimulant that makes one more alert and energetic, and causes loss of appetite and euphoria, so it helped the pirates stay up during their long hours of keeping watch. It is banned in most countries, but the Somalis seemed to have it incessantly. They wouldn't even wash it before eating, and ate it along with all the dirt it was covered in.

Out of curiosity, I once tried it while sitting with the pirates, but just couldn't take the taste after a point. SK and Bade kept asking if something was happening, but nothing did. We came to the conclusion that maybe we needed to have it like the Somalis—chewing it for hours and washing it down with extremely sweetened milk and tea. Maybe that was the key, but we really did not have the patience to sit and eat grass like goats.

The sequence of events leading up to my encounter with the gun started when I had gone for a routine check of the water levels in the tanks, an important step to ensure the stability of the ship. I was assigned the duty to check the levels in every tank. There was a rope with a copper weight tied to the end for this task—one would drop the rope through a narrow pipe into the tank and wait for the weight to touch the base. When one drew the rope back up, one could see how much of the rope was wet and estimate the water level in the tank. This procedure is called 'sounding' and has to be done every morning and evening for every tank.

The pirates, of course, thought this was a useless exercise. People who are not seafarers don't realize how much hard work it takes to keep a ship running. At the end of the day, a ship is a huge, complex machine and there are dozens of processes in every department that keep it functioning safely. The engineering and maintenance are as complex as an airplane's. Our ship was an old lady and things could go wrong pretty quickly.

In fact, the *RAK Afrikana* was scheduled to go to dry dock—a designated repair yard where ships have to go every few years for scheduled maintenance and repairs—upon completion of the voyage on which it was hijacked. There had been a hole in the hull a few months back and when we pulled into port it was attended to with proper facilities and equipment. Professional divers had welded it and got us seaworthy again.

But the pirates didn't have the intelligence to understand all this. For the first month, they hadn't let us check the water levels or run any sort of routine checks on deck and machinery at all. When they finally opened up to the idea, we requested for checks twice a day, but they only agreed to once, a few hours before sunset. And sounding duty had fallen on my young cadet shoulders.

That day, Jafar was on guard at the monkey island, the topmost open deck of the ship, which is the best spot for a lookout, thanks to its 360-degree view. This is the part of the ship where all the antennae for navigation and communication devices are installed, including the gyrocompass.

Just like every other day, before I started the sounding process, I had shown Jafar the rope and signalled that I was going, and he had given a faint nod of approval.

As I was nearing the end of the process, I heard Jafar shout, 'Aye!' Then, standing where he was, he pointed his gun at me. I was shocked and confused. At first, I thought he was doing this because there was some patrolling or warship movement, or some chopper was hovering close to us. But he told me to stay where I was and began climbing down the stairs towards me.

I hadn't been scared so far—I was doing something I used to do every day. But when I saw him rushing angrily towards me, I realized something was wrong. He didn't know a lot of English, so he said something in his language and then used hand movements to ask me what I was doing. I tried to explain, but he didn't understand. And then came a deadly sound— he loaded his AK-47 and brought it up to my forehead. As my heart sank, my hands went above my head instinctively. I closed my eyes and told myself this was the end for me. Even if he didn't shoot me, the gun was going to go off by mistake.

'Water come,' said Jafar. I understood that he thought I was punching a hole in the bottom of the ship.

'This check water level,' I replied, simplifying the syntax of my English for his benefit and showing him the wet rope with the weight attached to it. I tried to use other hand signals to explain exactly what I was doing there.

Jafar took the rope and acted as if the devil had taken hold of him. He struck the railing of the deck with the heavy copper weight, trying to prove that the rope was capable of breaking the ship's surfaces. Throughout these theatrics, the AK-47 remained pointed at my head.

I wasn't sure if Jafar had just been instructed by his bosses to intimidate us. There had been plenty of incidents in the previous two months when we were able to figure out that such instructions had been issued; they had led to different kinds of torture for us.

There was also the possibility that he really believed the copper weight could damage the ship, and that it was a conspiracy we were hatching to make us all go to land. The pirates probably thought the lowermost surface they could see was the bottom of the ship, and didn't understand that the bottom below the water line also had tanks and other spaces, not like that of their skiffs.

There was a third possibility too, that he was just having a bad trip from khat, or whatever he smoked, and needed some entertainment.

Luckily, Parjeet Singh Sodhi—a cut Surd, over six feet in height, fair-skinned, with chiselled arms, known among us as the Yuvraj Singh of the ship—saw this from the bridge, the area where all navigation duties were performed, akin to the cockpit on a plane. Parjeet was the Second Officer, the third-highest ranking officer in the hierarchy as deck officer, reporting directly to the captain, and he rushed down in time to save me. He shouted at Jafar, 'My friend!'

I was relieved to hear Parjeet's voice. It gave me some hope that I might survive this, but I did not dare turn my head or even look at him.

Jafar tried to explain to Parjeet what was happening and said the word 'hole' in English. Parjeet told him to relax, encouraged him by example to do some deep breathing, and with accompanying gestures said, 'You come up, we talk.'

This, finally, brought the situation under control. The entire ordeal had lasted a minute or two at most, but to me it felt like a lifetime. Jafar and Parjeet walked up to the bridge, but I stood still, trying to digest what had happened. I looked down to see if I had wet my pants; I hadn't. But it took me a while to get my breath back.

It was one of those days that made me think about what I had done to deserve this or why this was happening to me. My batchmates had only seen part of the incident, and asked me, '*Tune bhoot dekh liya kya* (Did you see a ghost)?' I told them what had happened.

The rest of the day continued to feel unusual. I tried to keep to myself. It took a while for my anxiety levels to drop, and after this incident, I stopped going for the sounding chore. In fact, nobody else wanted to do it after they came to know of what had happened. All of us agreed that we would attend to any danger if it arose. Some days later, water did flood the cargo holds, of which a ship can have many, depending on its size.

Everyone goes through some incident in life that completely changes them. For someone, it could be a car accident where they saw death up close. For others, it could be losing a loved one. For me, it was being hijacked by Somali pirates in the Indian Ocean.

Before this, I used to think life was easy. I was a boy with no plan, no focus and no goals. But being in a hijacked ship and living at gunpoint for close to a year made me realize the value of my life, figure out what was truly important to me and tune out everything else. It made me realize all the wrong decisions I had made, and how I could have been a better person, a better listener and a better learner. Most importantly, the question I repeatedly asked myself was how I could be a more honest human being.

In our culture, like many others around the world, family values are not taught formally—they are absorbed from our loved ones and the society we live in. I had taken them for granted as well. I thought I was financially secure and thus could take chances with my career. But instead, I came to realize how important it is to have somebody praying for you. As one of my instructors during pre-sea training days used to say, '*Agar aapke maa baap aapke saath hain, toh aapke liye dua ki kitaab khuli hai* (If your mother and father are with you, the book of prayers and good wishes is open for you).'

The stress that I went through, my family and friends went through, brought us much closer. All any of us could think about was me coming back home.

While in captivity, from time to time, I would pen down the events of the day in a notebook. I am not really sure why; it may have been because of the sheer amount of time I had on my hands. But maybe even back then, there was an idea in my head that if I ever got out of this alive, I would write a book about it. When the pirates saw me writing, they made me stop. They seriously thought I would write something on paper, put it in a bottle and let it float away across the ocean for someone to find!

Once, one of our officers was repeatedly writing a certain religious phrase on paper. He believed if he wrote it enough number of times, divine intervention would help us escape the ship. But the pirates made him stop too. When some of us cadets decided to spend our time studying, the pirates weren't okay with that either— they said they were illiterate and were 'still doing so well'. They told us to study about their religion instead, which they thought was the best thing to do.

I may not have been able to write about this back then, but it is time now.

Living on a hijacked ship, I saw everything from torture and humiliation to deprivation. I saw how money makes the world go around. I saw resilience and courage in the face of danger, but I also saw submission and defeat.

Sometimes, people describe what happened to us as 'kidnapping', but it's not the same. We weren't just picked up by some goons—we were sucked into an organized crime clique, who knew exactly what to do, how to do it and how much time every step should take. It was a smoothly run racket.

In all, twenty-four of us were hijacked and the only thing we prayed for was that all of us would get out safely. Unfortunately, not all twenty-four of us got off the ship alive. In fact, one of us was destined to not see freedom again. Even today, when I think about it, my hair stands on end.

But amid all that darkness, the one thing that was never snuffed out was the hope of getting to the end of our ordeal, going back home and seeing our families again. This is the story of that undying hope.

1

The Brat That I Was

There's no politically correct way to say this: Before becoming a seafarer, I was a brat. My family had moved out of India when I was eleven, and we lived in Bahrain and Oman when I was in my early teens. Then, one fine day, when I finished grade ten, my dad told us we were moving to the UAE. Financially, we were doing all right, and looking back, I realize that this had made me laid-back. Instead of going to a regular school for grades eleven and twelve, I registered for a three-year advanced diploma in engineering, to be followed by a three-year degree to complete my graduation in engineering. It had been my father's dream for both his sons to become engineers.

College was the first time I had easy access to booze. I had already tried cigarettes during my school days, but now, they, too, were more easily available. Even though officially I was still staying with my family, I was practically living in the hostel with my friends. My grades were okay and I wasn't getting into any trouble, so my family had no real issue with my life, or at least what they knew of it. And like any teenager, I made sure they didn't know all of it.

After my diploma, I managed to get admission to a university in Canada, and soon moved there. As usually happens with diasporic people, my initial circle comprised mostly of Indians. Around two months after landing in Canada, I was invited to a house party at a friend's house, with the promise of a good crowd, music and other stuff. Even before reaching the venue, I had had a few whiskeys and vodkas.

The house had a basement, a ground floor and a room on the first floor. There was a small backyard, the music was playing in the sitting area on the ground floor. Two people who had volunteered to be bartenders were making cocktails. There were also some chairs in the backyard where guests were smoking, and at the centre, to my surprise, sat a hookah. Coming from the Middle East to Canada, hookah had been sorely missed. In Canada, smoking indoors is illegal, as is drinking outdoors. But since we were at a private residence, no one was giving the laws a second thought. I also really liked the 'bring your own booze', or BYOB, culture of house parties in Canada. Guests would leave whatever they brought at the bar and go refill their own glasses throughout, and by the end of the night, the leftovers would be mashed together into a cocktail, and you would be hammered.

As I walked to the backyard with my drink, I saw one of the guys (who I came to know was Persian) standing at the door smoking hookah. He asked me if I would like to take a drag, and I asked him what flavour it was, but he just smiled mysteriously. That should've been a warning sign, but I was intrigued, and because I was already experienced with a hookah, I thought, how bad could it be?

A bunch of us stood in a circle, taking drags by turn. When it came to me, I took one drag, then another, and then a third. I remember smiling before passing it on to the next person. Then, another round completed, I took another long drag. And then another. And then another. A few more rounds went by.

The girl standing opposite me asked if this was my first time smoking a hookah, and I bragged about my hookah days back in the Middle East. She flashed me a cute smile and I felt flattered. She expressed her concern that I was mixing drinks and the hookah, but I told her I was feeling okay. She later told me that I had been far from okay, swaying left and right while I said all this.

The next thing I knew, the drink in my hand slipped and smashed on the floor, and as I bent down to try and sort out the mess, I lost my balance, caught hold of the railing behind me, but still tumbled to the floor.

Some guys helped me up, took me inside and lay me down on the couch. Heavy electronic music was playing in the background—it was probably psychedelic trance, with neon lights flashing in the room from different directions. I just couldn't control the high. However, I still have a memory of looking at the ceiling and not being able to see anything; I don't think I understood if the room was too dark or my eyes were just partially open. Suddenly, I felt as if I badly needed fresh air, so I picked myself up and went to the porch.

The temperature outside was minus three or four degrees Celsius. It was close to 1 in the morning and I was wearing just a T-shirt, jeans and socks. I fell on to the grass and announced, 'Call the cops!' My roommate, who had come along with me and was a little less intoxicated, completely freaked out. I repeated myself several times, but he also seemed to be barely in his senses.

We had been invited to the party (which was at someone else's house) by a Punjabi guy called Jogi whom I had befriended, and at this point, he walked out of the house, looked at me and went, '*Behen chod, kuchh nahin hua, ghar jaa ke so jaa, theek ho jayega* (Fucker, nothing's wrong, go home and sleep, you'll be fine).'

This was going to be no joke, because the university dorm was five kilometres up the hill, and this was long before Uber existed. Jogi, an interesting dude who enjoyed writing songs and wanted nothing more than to get 'fixed' in Canada (meaning citizenship), helped me up off the ground and decided to accompany me and my roommate on our way.

I was too numb to feel anything in that horrid weather, and I just remember seeing the street lights around me as we walked. My brain was still fried and I was unable to process much—most of what I've recounted so far was filled in by others over the course of the next day or so.

Somehow, around 4 a.m., we reached the dorm, but we initially couldn't find the keys to the room. All three of us were in a bad condition by that point—I was blabbering and making no sense, while Jogi and my roommate were also intoxicated and tired of helping me up the hill.

Finally, once the key was found and we got inside, I told Jogi to crash right there for the night, and he immediately grabbed a chair and straightened his legs, saying he would leave as soon as he felt a bit less tired. I told him I was going to the washroom.

Jogi woke up around 6, and realized he had slept longer than intended. But when he looked at my bed, it was empty. He thought I might have gone to the washroom again, so he waited for a while. But when I still did not come out, he peeked in through the open washroom door and glimpsed my hand on the floor. Panicking, he rushed outside and returned with the floor's proctor (a student on each floor who was like a hall monitor—a designated person for emergencies). They saw that while my left hand was on the floor, the right was on the closed lid of the toilet, as was my head. I had been snoring in that position for over two hours. The proctor's first reaction was to click a picture of me for his 'collection', and then he helped Jogi lift me up and put me in bed. I stayed passed out through all this.

That was how my journey in Canada began, but thankfully, things got better. Gradually, I built a friends' circle, not only because I could gel with people easily, but also thanks to my skill as a cook, especially when it came to meat. Whenever friends wanted to have mutton, they would call me; I would tell them to get the mutton and I would cook it. That way, I got to party without paying anything.

The association of Indian students at the university had just expanded and rebranded itself as a community for all 'desi' individuals, and now featured Bangladeshi,

Sri Lankan and other nationalities as well. This helped me make friends across cultural lines, as did my connection to the Middle East and the fact that I had arrived from Dubai, which got me in among the Emiratis, Qataris, Bahrainis, Saudis and Omanis.

One of the other notable parties I was invited to took place around Diwali. I was part of the organizing crew and got enlisted as a volunteer so I would not have to pay for tickets. I was tasked with being the first to arrive and the last to leave, to ensure the party went off smoothly.

But it wouldn't be a party without a drinking competition, and sure enough, there was a competition to see who could gulp down the most shots. I came in third. While I was still on my feet and continued to enjoy myself, I went to the dance floor and was soon joined by a girl, who asked me, 'How come you are not sloshed?'

I had learnt my lesson from that first party in Canada, and this time around didn't brag about anything. 'The trick to drinking is to hydrate adequately,' was my one-line reply to her question. The girl smiled. She was from Bangladesh, and looked interesting. She was a very good dancer, and probably thanks to the alcohol in my blood, I matched her step for step. Like every desi party, there had to be a partners' dance in the end, with a free round of drinks for whoever won. Needless to say, the Bangladeshi girl and I won, and since she was a teetotaller, I ended up savouring the free beer she won as well. We exchanged numbers before parting ways for the evening, and went on to become close friends.

Whenever I was at her place, I used to cook for her. But mostly, I was a very outgoing person back then. We would meet often for coffee and later I would carry on to friends' places for parties, or just go out for a late-night dinner. I was having the time of my life.

Now, many years later, my way of unwinding is simply a long drive, or driving and camping at quiet places outside the city hustle with my wife and my dog.

By the end of the semester, things began to go downhill. Canada was my first taste of total freedom, even though there hadn't been many restrictions back home. I was partying hard, maybe too much, and forgetting there were other things that needed to be taken care of too.

It got to a point where a day before my end-term exams, I didn't know the subject I was supposed to study for the next day. Jogi and my roommate also partied hard, but unlike me, they seemed to know when to stop. Jogi was a hard-working guy and my roommate was smart, so they both had their ways to get the grades they needed.

A few days later, in the middle of the end-term exams, an Arab friend called me over to his place. I hesitated but he was insistent and promised to wrap things up early, so I went. He served an expertly made hookah with a smile on his face; by now, I had learnt to handle these things. But we ended up getting carried away and losing track of time. Sitting out there in the cold, my friend started talking in Arabic, and I had no idea what he was saying. So, I started speaking to him in Hindi. And there we sat, laughing our guts out, not understanding a word of what we were saying to each other.

Just then, the surroundings went extremely quiet, and the first snowflakes of the season started falling. I put my finger on my lips to ensure that the stillness was not broken, and I got to experience snowfall for the first time. I knew I should really be studying, but I couldn't help but sit and admire the beauty of the snow, and the silence that accompanied it. I still crave that moment of peace.

The exam results brought me back to my senses. They were embarrassing, to say the least; until then, I had always ensured my grades stayed up. I realized things had gone too far, and called up my family to admit that this may not be the right place for me. I told them I should come back and do something more productive.

I started wrapping up my life in Canada, and telling my friends it was time to go. They also knew I had let things go too far; they all told me to take a break and hoped I would come back. But I knew this chapter was over. While packing my bags, I realized this was the first time I had failed at something. That brought tears to my eyes, and pushed all the arrogance, all the ego, all the showing off to the back burner. It had been my decision to go to Canada and prove myself, and I had failed miserably. Till this day, I wish I had gotten a hold on myself and the situation.

On my long flight back to Dubai, I thought hard about how to broach the subject with my family. Even at my lowest moment, my father had ensured I had the quickest connecting flights back home, without any long airport layovers. It was the first time I began noticing the small things parents do for their children. I had nothing to say to him, except that I was sorry. I was ready to make up for my failure in Canada in whatever way my family wanted me to—even if they told me to wash dishes at a restaurant.

I was nervous about what lay ahead. I just hoped my father would have a solution.

2

Life at Sea

I landed in Dubai anxious and confused, and my father was there alone at the airport to receive me. He's always been a reserved person and didn't say much on the way home, except asking if everything had been okay on the flight and if I wanted to stop at McDonald's on the way.

I was expecting to at least receive a tongue-lashing or be grounded for the money I had flushed down the drain. But to my surprise, the reception at home was normal. My mother welcomed me with a big hug, and I saw she had prepared all my favourite dishes. I could see glimpses of sadness on my parents' faces, but they actively helped me cheer up.

At long last I smiled, and it dawned on me that nothing was more important to parents than their children's happiness. When we live under their roof and they say no to something we want, they do it not to be strict, but for our own well-being. In fact, far from taking me to task, my father even asked me if I wanted to go back to Canada and give it another try.

But I didn't want that, and instead began worrying about what I would do next.

For the first time, I had a proper goal—to do well in the future and not be dependent on my parents. However, I had no plan. Two or three days after my return, when my father asked me what my plan was, I felt guilty and told him I'd do whatever he wanted me to, even wait tables.

He suggested a career in the merchant navy. He told me about the training ship and warned that it would be hard work. '*Beta, bahut mehnat karni hogi. Bathroom bhi saaf karna hoga. Woh sab kaam karne padenge jo abhi tak soche bhi nahin hain* (Son, you'll have to work very hard. Even clean the toilets. You'll have to do things you never imagined yourself doing).'

I had figured out he would always have my best interests at heart, so I promised I would do all that he was saying without batting an eyelid. It was a completely alien career choice for my family—no relative, close or distant, had been in the merchant navy.

The programme my father was talking about was affiliated to a maritime school in New Zealand and a training school in the UAE, so I would receive dual degrees. I had to complete my 'pre-sea' in the UAE on board the training ship—these are theory studies for a fixed duration that one needs to complete before joining any ship for sea service. Then, there would be about seventeen months of sea time before my first exam, which would be for a navigation officer's licence. The other option would be to complete the sea time, appear for theory exams and get a bachelor's degree without the sailing licence.

So, there I was, all set to be a sailor, looking forward to the small stipend I would be paid for my sea time. I had made up my mind, and there was no looking back.

My pre-sea went quite well; the instructors gave good feedback about me. Upon its completion, there was still some time in hand to start the cadetship onboard and I had come to India to visit my grandparents and parallelly do Basic Safety Training courses, which were mandatory before joining any ship. Soon, it was time to board my first ship, along with two of my batchmates, SK and Bade. We were to fly from Mumbai to Addis Ababa in Ethiopia, and then join the ship on the island of Zanzibar in Tanzania.

Before I left, my mother had some words of advice for me, '*Itni duur jaa raha hai* (You're going so far). We won't even be able to talk every day. Take care and don't fight with anyone.'

On 16 September 2009, a calm day at sea, I boarded the *RAK Afrikana* in Zanzibar. From a sailor's point of view, our ship didn't belong to a very well-known company—it was part of a small fleet. I later found out that the shipping industry was still grappling with the after-effects of the 2008 financial crisis.

Our on-board commanding officer was Capt. Rameshwar Naithani (or Capt. Ram, as everyone called him), a five-foot-ten, dark-skinned, broad-shouldered man in his mid-fifties, who had been at sea for more than thirty years. He had been away from sailing for the last five years, but had had to return after facing losses in business. Despite his age, he moved swiftly, like a young lad.

Once familiarized with the ship and crew in Zanzibar, we sailed to Moroni in the beautiful island country of Comoros, off the eastern coast of Africa. Our task was pretty straightforward—discharge the remaining cargo—but I was super excited about it. Our cargo watches followed a six-hours-on, six-hours-off schedule, and I didn't think twice before going ashore and exploring the place during my rest hours. Even if I didn't go out, I still ensured we were having a good time on board. I had taken along a PlayStation console, some games, speakers and a small TV. The cabins allotted to my batchmates and me became the 'chill zone' on the ship, where everyone came for a smoke, and alcohol flowed freely.

On one occasion, and this was before Parjeet had joined us as Second officer, we had just sailed out of a port fully stocked with the ship's supplies and our own. I had to assist the 0000hrs to 0400hrs night watch, which meant I had to report for duty at 2345hrs (unlike cargo watch, navigation watch is four hours twice a day and as cadets we sometimes assisted during both the watches or just once at night, depending on the deck work scheduled during the day). The process was simple—reach fifteen minutes before your watch starts, take over from the cadet on duty, get your eyes adjusted to the dim lights on the bridge, complete your four hours efficiently while maintaining a safe passage, and hand over to the next guy. But by the time I was to relieve one of the senior cadets from bridge duty, I had gotten so drunk at the encouragement of my shipmates' chants of '*ek aur, ek aur* (one more, one more)' that I didn't even wake up. The senior cadet came to wake me up and I said sleepily, '*Haan, jaa raha hoon* (Yes, I'm going).' As soon as he left, I fell asleep again.

An hour passed, and the senior cadet, Khan (Zaheer Khan), had to extend his watch by an hour. The then Second Officer came back again to wake me up, but I couldn't be bothered. Then, to my bad luck, the main engine suddenly stopped. Capt. Ram came to the bridge, saw the Second Officer all by himself, and asked, 'Where is the cadet on duty?' He got the answer, 'Never showed up.' This, of course, did not go down well with the Captain. He then asked, '*Kaun hai* cadet (Who is the cadet)?', and the Second Officer replied. '*Naya waala* (The new one).'

The Second Officer came back to my cabin and splashed water on my face. He told me, 'The Captain is on the bridge, come now.' I got a hold on myself, washed my face and quickly brushed my teeth and gargled, but was still reeking of alcohol when I reached the bridge. Capt. Ram was plotting the ship's position on the chart, which was standard practice and one of the first things taught at pre-sea. He looked at me and asked if I had been sleeping—I said yes—and asked me to plot the position of the ship. The GPS was in front of me, and I had the latitude and longitude. I just had to plot the coordinates in front of me. Normally, I could plot positions with my eyes closed, but now I tried thrice, and each time the position came out on land!

The Captain shouted, '*Kya kar raha hai, behen chod* (What are you doing, fucker)?' This last one was his favourite word, being as he was a sailor and a man from Delhi. The word was uttered so often that even the Zanzibar crew knew what it meant. The Captain spoke it regardless of whether he was feeling good, bad, kind or angry; it was left to the recipient to understand from his tone what his emotion was in that moment. At this moment, I felt as if he was about to pick me up like the Incredible Hulk would, and fling me over the rails. He walked to the chart table and took the parallel ruler from me and plotted the position himself. By then, he had smelt the alcohol on me. '*Chutiye, daaru pee rakhi hai* (Fucker, you're drunk)?' he asked. I said, 'Yes sir.'

He then told me to go to the telegraph (a device with a lever that signals the engine room about the speed the bridge wants), put it on 'stop engine', and 'fuck off from the bridge'.

The next day was a Sunday and my troubles didn't stop. I woke up with a heavy head and was sitting in the officers' mess room (a merchant ship has separate mess rooms or dining rooms for officers and crew) gulping down water, when I was called in again by the Captain on the bridge.

'Sir, you were looking for me?' I ventured.

Capt. Ram looked at me and repeated my words with sarcasm. He then said, 'Yes, I'm the Captain and I am looking for you!'

Someone had complained that the new boys on board—SK, Bade and I—were partying and playing loud music late every night. This wasn't untrue—we used to listen to all sorts of music depending on our moods and alcohol levels, from electronic to rock, Punjabi, Hindi and even Nusrat Fateh Ali Khan's qawwalis.

Capt. Ram gave me a piece of his mind. 'Have you come here to party? You don't respect the culture of this ship, you don't respect your seniors. I've been on ships for so many years and even I haven't stepped on the bridge after drinking! Spoilt brats!' he spat.

He finally let me off with one last warning, that if there was no improvement, I would be signed off, which means sent home from the next port.

If I got signed off before time, all my hard work would come to zilch, and my career would be back to square one. It would be Canada all over again. And the worst part was that he was right. It was unacceptable for me to go to the bridge in that condition. I needed to pull up my socks.

Much has been said about the lives of sailors, and my story so far is doing nothing to improve that image. It seems an easy life, with all the tales of women at ports and flowing alcohol. Sailors coming back home always have long hair or a beard, which gives them a rockstar look. In reality, it's one of the toughest jobs around, and hence very well paid. The stories about sailors are just yarns; once on board, you hardly get time to think of all these things, given your responsibilities out at sea.

I remember when Abdullah, our Bosun, the head of the crew in charge of deck maintenance, work allocation and deck stores inventory, decided to share some pearls of wisdom with me. The Bosun (or Boatswain) is one of the most important ranks for a cadet to learn from, and we had to make sure we remained in his good books. Abdullah himself was quite well read and used to share his collection of books with us. The Zanzibar crew looked up to him because he was the most educated among them.

We were on the ship, having a tea break with a smoke, when Abdullah said, 'When you go to any club in Tanzania, especially Zanzibar, you keep all your cash in your pocket and you keep your wallet on the table, next to your beer. That's how you get everyone's attention.'

I asked why, and he replied, 'You go to a club as a seafarer, and you must show everybody that you are loaded with cash. That's why you keep your wallet out. You don't go there, place your order and check your wallet for five or ten dollars. You tell them to open a tab, and that you are sitting here. Then you see the attention you get.'

I tried this, and it worked.

While the six-hours-on, six-hours-off schedule seemed great in the beginning, in terms of having some fun ashore, within three or four months, it was taking a toll on my resting hours, and so I barely left the ship any more. The more you remain on the ship, the more responsibility you are given, and on top of that, if you're trying to become more attentive towards your duties and minor details, time just starts to fly. If I had to go out, I would just go to an internet café to check e-mails, grab a meal and get back quickly.

For a cadet, the first time crossing the Equator is a big deal, and comes with a specific ritual attached. As we approached the Equator for my first time, my seniors were super excited about the ritual aspect of it. We were supposed to cross the 0 degree latitude after midnight, and all three of us new cadets were asked to gather at the monkey island and watch for boats patrolling the Equator. We had no clue what these were, and due to the excitement didn't even think this was practically impossible. It was one of those sailor pranks that seniors play on juniors when they are fresh onboard.

Anyway, I had a 0400hrs to 0800hrs watch with Ali Baig (Chief Officer—deck officer second in command after the Captain) in the morning. After my dinner that night, I was in two minds about whether to be awake and wait until the patrolling boats appeared or go to bed and catch up on my beauty sleep and come in fresh at 0400hrs. I also remembered Capt. Ram's warning to me from the previous time when I had messed up during the night watch. Hence, I decided to skip the patrolling boats, unlike SK and Bade, who had impeccable timing. Since Bade was taking over the night shift from SK at midnight, the poor guys had to stand on the monkey island in pitch darkness and cold, binoculars in hand, waiting for the patrolling boats to appear. But since I didn't show up, the senior cadet who had planned the prank punished all three of us by shaving our heads. This is a perfect example of how when one fucks up, all have to take the hit. You get complimented together and you get punished together. It's part of the learning that aboard a ship, teamwork is always the mantra, not individual competency.

Being on a foreign-going vessel, one good part was that we got to visit different countries, with Pakistan being one of them. Going to Pakistan was always an interesting experience with Indians on the crew, because someone or the other would end up having strong nationalist sentiments. Bade was one such person, who claimed, '*Wahan ka toh main namak bhi nahin khaaunga* (I won't even have their salt).' He was resolved to not set foot on Pakistani soil. I, on the other hand, had lived in Dubai and other Gulf cities, so I had Pakistani friends.

The great leveller turned out to be the biryani from a restaurant at the Karachi port—even Bade forgot his misplaced patriotism in the face of that aroma and taste.

But there was, of course, the problem of hiding alcohol from customs, because Pakistan is officially dry. If even a drop of booze was found, it would have become a challenge, especially given that the Captain and a lot of the crew were from India. We had to be extra careful.

When the customs guys came aboard, dressed in their salwar-kameez and jackets, I escorted them to the ship's office, which was a room next to the Captain's cabin where all formalities and paperwork were attended to whenever a third party came onboard.

At any other port, Capt. Ram wore a formal white shirt and black trousers, but this time, he was in full uniform, including peak cap, tie and epaulettes. He usually greeted customs officials with a 'good morning' or a 'good day', depending on the time, but here, he said 'namaskar', dripping with patriotism, which gave me goosebumps.

I guess this made the customs guys more determined to find something, and they started going through the ship. David John, one of the senior cadets, used an old whiskey bottle made of glass for his daily water needs, and it hadn't struck him that even an empty liquor bottle could be a problem. It was perhaps his bad luck that on his floor, the customs guys asked to open only his room, saw the bottle and lost their minds. We tried to explain, but they refused to understand, and said they couldn't touch or taste the liquid to check if we were telling the truth. David, whom the bottle belonged to, got an earful for this, and we all had to work long hours to compensate. As I mentioned earlier, that's how life out at sea is: one mistake by an individual, and the whole team pays for it to resolve it. It's not easy—the smallest mistake can lead to end of life and nobody from outside the ship can save you.

We were supposed to leave for Seychelles, but we were delayed in Karachi due to slow cargo operations. Finally upon our arrival in Seychelles, we were taken in to berth, but brought back out to anchorage (an area of sea outside the port where ships await their turn at the berths). The reason they gave us was that 'big fat rats' had found their way into the cargo hold. Generally, this can become a big issue at any port, upon shifting from berth and sent to the anchorage, where we had to fumigate the whole ship. A port-authorized team was sent to put rat-kill formulas and traps. But it rained heavily that day and all the rat kill got washed away. We never found any rats, but in the next two days, we were called inside the port again to discharge the cargo.

When we finally set foot on Seychelles, I decided to go to shore for a few hours. I happened to meet some good people there, made a phone call home, checked my e-mails and had amazing fish and chips with a couple of pints of chilled beer.

Why I remember this port call so clearly after so many years is because it turned out to be my last moment of freedom for a very long time.

Sometimes you just fall in love with a place, and that's how it was with Seychelles, so when the time came to depart, we all hoped that everything had gone well with the recipient of the cargo. That way, in the future, we would have more chances to visit Seychelles. It would be so nice to explore the nightlife next time or drive around this small but stunning island.

Our next destination was Zanzibar, which was three or four days away. Once the pilot (a person designated by the country the ship is entering or leaving, who helps the ship navigate the port without difficulties) disembarked from our ship after crossing the channel, and I was securing the gangway, the only thing on my mind was that junior cadets were supposed to join us on board in Zanzibar. The predator was savouring the thought of prey before he got his hands on them, so to speak.

On the way to Zanzibar, there was barely any deck work because there were still lots of containers there. The next three days would just be watch-keeping. A few of our Zanzibari crew members were also supposed to sign off at their home port. Parjeet had joined us as the new Second Officer from Karachi, who, too, had been a cadet for the same company, a few batches senior to us. At times, I felt he had been sent to set an example for us. But this left Kuldeep Singh, the Third Officer, a little unhappy because he had not been promoted, and somebody much younger had come and taken charge as Second Officer.

A day or so after setting sail from Seychelles, our engine broke down. The engine had been due for some repairs, but we hadn't had the time to get them done in Seychelles because of the rat fiasco.

It was another Sunday, and I was looking forward to relaxing. I thought the halt would just be for a few hours and that we would be back on our way before lunch.

Life was good here, out on the beautiful, open seas. Fresh air and calm, clean water all around. I was standing on deck with a cup of steaming coffee in my hand, the cool breeze washing over me. I was half an hour late, so had missed the morning conversation with Muhammed, our Chief Cook, as he had gotten busy with breakfast preps. Things couldn't be more stable after all the turmoil in Canada. Mentally, I was in a good space.

But destiny had other plans.

3

The Hijacking

Sunday, 11 April 2010, was supposed to be a relaxed day on board the *RAK Afrikana*. It had almost been seven months since I had boarded the ship, and as we cadets were having breakfast, our Chief Officer, Ali Baig, and the Bosun, Abdullah, came in and asked us to volunteer for some deck work that would last until morning tea.

The Chief Officer was a Pakistani man in his mid-forties. He was short, thin, had grey hair and a low-maintenance moustache, and would be found with a cigarette in his hand about 90 per cent of the time. The Chief Officer's role on a ship is not an easy one—the position comes with the heaviest workload, the biggest parts of which are deck maintenance and cargo planning. Ali Baig loved his orange overalls (jumpsuits that are common as work wear on ships), whose sleeves and pant legs would always be folded because of his diminutive stature.

When we were told about the deck work, we cadets were really disheartened, because on Sundays, you weren't expected to do much deck work, especially when the ship was out at sea and not at a port. Usually, we would finish our watchkeeping, do other routine chores and rest.

My Sundays were made fun by Muhammed, who never disappointed when I would ask for a different style of eggs than the usual. On this particular Sunday, we had asked him for French toast. But the Chief Officer's request meant that we would be eating less, since we had to report on deck right after breakfast for cargo lashing. This is a hard but very important task, in which steel chains are used to secure the cargo to prevent movement or shifting during sailing, which could damage the structure of the ship or the surrounding cargo. A big shift in weight could even lead to an unstable ship.

At half past eight, the Bosun, as always, assigned us our individual jobs, and I was told to go and watch the fo'c'sle (or forecastle) area. Remember in the film *Titanic* where the characters Jack and Rose stand with their arms spread wide, feeling the breeze on their faces and kindling their romance? That's the fo'c'sle. And I stood there by myself in grease-and-oil-stained overalls, safety gloves and helmet, ensuring everything was secure, as far removed from romance as possible.

I was doing my usual checks when I heard something that sounded like a car backfiring. I ignored it, thinking it probably came from our welder Lucas's gun, as he was on deck with us that morning. I had never heard a gunshot before, so I didn't know what it sounded like.

But then, the sound rang out twice more, and suddenly, I heard commotion and turned around to see the crew running towards the accommodation area. Senior Cadet Zaheer was running from the starboard section (the right side of the ship when facing the bow), head ducked, to the port section (the left side of the ship), and I ran after him, wanting to ask what was going on.

I could hear and see Third Officer Kuldeep Singh on the bridge wing, which is an open deck walking area right outside the bridge, extending out over both the port and starboard sections of the ship. He looked down at the crew and asked, 'Boss, *kya ho gaya hai* (What is happening)?' Kuldeep was a slim, tall fellow with long legs. He was always clean-shaven and had an equal mix of grey and black hair. He had a slight hunch but that was probably because of his height. He was the officer on watch; it was his duty to keep a proper radar and visual lookout in the area of the world we were currently drifting in. A radar watch is one of the most important tasks on the ship for a navigating officer, as it helps track other ships' movements to navigate a safe passage. Along with this, a visual lookout is mandatory, especially when the engine is not operational and the ship is drifting.

I ducked and started running towards the accommodation, still confused, when someone screamed: 'Piracy attack!'

That was when Kuldeep, who was still on the port-side bridge wing, realized what was happening and raised the emergency alarm. I went to the bridge, as I had learnt during my last emergency drill duties, and saw Capt. Ram and Second Officer Parjeet Singh Sodhi walk in. Kuldeep could barely speak and stammered, 'Sir... sir, pirates... pirates!'

The Captain asked, 'Where are they?'

Parjeet told him they were right alongside us on the starboard side, but they were still in their boat.

Our ship's engine was still not operational, as one of the cylinder heads was being serviced. Capt. Ram called the engine room from the intercom placed behind the telegraph, hoping the engineers could get it ready, but was told that it would take another half an hour to assemble it back. The Captain asked if the engineers could at least give it 'just a kick', which could create some waves around the ship, which could topple the pirates' skiff or at least disturb them, so that we could have a little time in hand. Their boat was extremely small, and when the sea is calm, this is worth a try.

Our ship's cargo occupancy was at 70 per cent of capacity, since we had already discharged some in Seychelles. Because of that, the ship's freeboard (the distance between the water line and the main deck) had increased further. The design of our ship was such that with cargo at 30 per cent below full capacity, the pirates still had to climb at least five to six metres from their boat to the deck. Doing that with the help of a rope would have been impossible if the ship was moving at ten to twelve knots, but if it was floating or drifting like it was now, the task was doable.

However, the engine room control had bad news for the Captain—there was no chance of a kick. Capt. Ram slammed the receiver down in desperation and uttered '*behen chod*'. We were dead ducks now.

The pirates tried to throw a hook on to our railing, and it took a few attempts before it caught. Then, for a while, we heard no more sounds, before suddenly, a face appeared from behind a container. As soon as one guy was on board, it was over for us; there was not much we could do after that. There had been four or five of them on the skiff.

A second pirate soon came on board, and the two of them moved towards the accommodation area, holding up guns and treading slowly, keeping themselves alert for any surprise attack.

Parjeet, who was monitoring from the bridge window at the front end a few floors above the pirates on the deck, confirmed this to Capt. Ram, who was on the satellite phone in the chart room trying to reach the ship's owner. 'Sir, two armed pirates on board,' said the Second Officer, keeping his eyes on the pirates. The Captain immediately walked back near the telegraph and picked up the intercom again, called the engine room and ordered the personnel there to go join the other crew in the 'citadel'. This is a safe room with emergency communication equipment and basic supplies like food and water, which had been mandated by international guidelines for every ship crossing a high-risk area since the rise in piracy.

Amid so much chaos, I felt numb and forgot what I was supposed to be doing here, but looking at Capt. Ram and Parjeet taking quick steps one after the other, I came back to my senses. I was sitting underneath the very high frequency (VFH) radio communication equipment, so I raised the distress call. I pressed the SOS button and said, 'Mayday! Mayday! Mayday! This is *RAK Afrikana*, IMO 8200553. We are under piracy attack. We have two armed pirates on board. I repeat, two armed pirates on board.'

I repeated this again and again, along with our latitude and longitude position (the specifics of which, unfortunately, have been driven out of my memory by the passage of time). We were hoping to get a quick response and make the pirates vanish.

Capt. Ram then rushed to the starboard bridge wing. This is when I peeked from the bridge window and caught sight of one of the pirates. They must have been at sea for fifteen or twenty days, judging by his condition. He was wearing a vest with holes in it, and a lungi or some kind of sheet wrapped around his lower body; his feet were bare and his eyes wide open. He was carrying a gun on his right shoulder and was looking towards the bridge. As soon as he saw the Second Officer, he pointed the gun at him. By this time, a third guy had joined their raiding party.

Capt. Ram tried to tell the pirates that it was a dead ship, with a broken engine. He told them there was a hole in the ship, and they wouldn't get anything from it. But the pirates didn't listen. One of them used his gun to signal to the Captain to come down. Third Officer Kuldeep, now sitting down and panting, asked, '*Kya ho raha hai* (What's happening)?' He was shitting bricks at this point, as was I.

Capt. Ram used the ship's announcement system to communicate with everyone in the accommodation and citadel. 'If you all can hear me, the vessel has been hijacked at the moment. We have raised a distress call. Please stay put in the citadel. Do not move out until we tell you to. We have three pirates on board as of now. They are armed. Don't try to be a hero. We have called for help. Let's hope for the best. Stay safe,' he announced.

By now, the pirates were getting impatient and kept repeating 'come down'. They wanted someone to escort them up. They fired a few shots in the air, and Parjeet volunteered to go down. He descended the stairs slowly, with his hands in the air, ensuring the pirates saw he was unarmed. The pirates did not let him come close, and as he reached the cargo deck, they asked him to stop, turn around and walk. He went back up the stairs, followed by the gun-toting pirates.

I got a close look at them for the first time, and they all looked strikingly similar, except for their different heights. They were extremely skinny, had similar hairdos, yellow-tinged and jaundiced-looking eyes, yellow teeth and dirty nails. Their lungis and feet were wet, because their skiff was tiny and would've been spraying up water. Given their builds, we could've easily outnumbered them and beaten them up. Heck, Abdullah the Bosun alone could've taken all three of them down. But they had guns, and we didn't.

On the bridge of every ship, hanging on a wall, you'll find its design layout, known as the general arrangement plan. You'll also find the crew list, with the total number of persons on board and their ranks. The pirates seemed as illiterate as anyone you could come across, but were well versed in making sense of these practical things. They looked at the plan and checked for everything that could go wrong. They counted the ones on the bridge and told everyone else to come there too. Then, they pushed us to get the others out of the citadel and in front of them. Their commander, whom I later got to know was named Abdi, said we had better hurry. The crew reluctantly came to the bridge, and the space got extremely crowded.

The pirates held their guns close and kept them pointed at us. The crew stood and walked in a queue. The pirates did a few headcounts to be sure nobody was missing or hiding. It was ironic that at this point in time, they were as concerned about our whole crew as Capt. Ram was.

Satisfied, Abdi smiled and then shouted, 'Ship go Somalia now!'

Our Chief Engineer, Zulfikar Shareef, who hailed from Pakistan, tried to intervene. Shareef, whom everyone called 'Bada Sahab', was the most experienced on board—a light-complexioned man with white hair, a matching long beard and a slight hump in his neck and shoulder region. He greeted the pirates with a 'salaam' and told them they could see for themselves that our engine was completely dismantled and needed repairs. There was a big communication gap and he tried to use the word '*makina*', which is Arabic for 'machine', meaning engine in this context. Abdi replied, 'I'm engineer. Shut up! Go start engine. We go Somalia now!'

Capt. Ram and Chief Officer Ali Baig also joined the conversation and tried to reason with Abdi some more, but it didn't help. Baig said everyone knew the Horn of Africa was a dangerous area, so why would we stop here if we had anything of value? This was when Abdi took two steps forward, stood in front of Capt. Ram and Baig, looked the Captain directly in the eye and put one finger close to his lips. 'Sshh ... I am Captain now. You cross my country, you pay tax, or I kill.'

They now made us all kneel. One of the other pirates standing beside Abdi had an unusual twitching around his left eye and upper cheek. It was hard to not notice it, but I tried my best to look away. Unfortunately, one of my senior cadets, Sandeep Singh, could not. He kept looking at the pirate's eye, wondering what was wrong with it. The pirate noticed the stare and said, 'What you look?' Sandeep replied, 'Nothing.' But before Sandeep could say another word, he got kicked on the shoulder. Everybody around him yelled so loudly that his own scream of pain couldn't be heard. I was right next to Sandeep, and felt the force of the kick as he crashed on top of me. When I later asked Sandeep why the fuck he had been staring at the pirate, he told me he had thought the guy had been winking at him.

Just then, we heard the unmistakable whir of a helicopter hovering somewhere nearby. Abdi immediately ordered his two cohorts to cover the port and starboard bridge wing entrances and look out for it. He issued this instruction in their own language, but it was easy to figure out. We were all told to sit and stay in our positions. They looked outside, communicated something with each other and then called for Capt. Ram. Parjeet was sitting close to Abdi, so he was also grabbed and taken outside to the starboard bridge wing. There was a small hope that this would end now—maybe the people in the chopper would be able to scare them off, or negotiate our release.

Instead, the pirates made a statement of their own to the people in the chopper—they made Capt. Ram and Parjeet kneel and aimed the guns at their heads. The officers were made to raise their arms above their heads, then hit with the gun butts. The pirates were making it clear that they had taken over the ship, and soon we could hear the whir of the rotor blades growing fainter and fainter as the helicopter flew away, and took our hopes with it.

I wanted to ask my crewmates what was going to happen next: Would they accept some money and let us go? Could we negotiate a deal with them? There were so many thoughts running through my head, but I didn't dare utter a word in front of the gun-toting pirates. I wanted to call home and speak to my parents, and tell my mother, 'Don't worry, I will come back. Don't wait up for me like you used to at night, because this may take longer.'

Soon, two more pirates came on the bridge, taking the number up to five. One of the new guys was really short and had wide eyes like those of a drunk, even though he wasn't. He was the only one who carried a thick stick instead of a gun. Despite the tension in the air, I joked to myself that he must be the pirates' cadet. His name was Hamood.

To make it easier to manage the crew, the pirates made us disperse to different places—some were sent to the engine room, some to the crew mess room, while some remained on the bridge. I was sent to the mess room with the rest of the cadets, some crew members, Abdullah, Kuldeep and Baig. Hamood the 'cadet pirate', as I thought of the short guy, kept watch over us.

The pirates who were going to the engine room looked quite scared, almost as if they were going to a haunted place. This wasn't surprising, because to someone new to a ship, a space like the engine room would be a hot, smelly, noisy maze, and someone from the crew could hide behind the huge machines and overpower the pirates. They knew they were vulnerable there, so they instructed the engineers to fix the engine in thirty minutes and make it ready to sail.

About a little over an hour into the hijacking, Hassan Idris, our oiler, who was with me in the mess room, wanted to go to the toilet. He seemed to have been holding it in for a while and said the word 'washroom'. Hamood didn't know the word and refused to let him go. But I remembered the Arabic word, worked up some courage and said, 'Hamam.' Hamood looked at me with suspicious eyes but didn't respond. I wasn't sure if he understood or acted not to understand or was suspicious of me speaking Arabic. The pirate wasn't in the mood to let anyone out of his sight, and offered Hassan a can. Abdullah intervened and tried to reason with him.

While all this was going on, suddenly the lights went out. It seemed like the generator, which runs independently of the engine, had tripped. We were scared, though still calm, but pandemonium ensued. Hamood was much more scared than we realized; we couldn't see him but we could hear him get up, pick up his stick and try to get to the mess room door desperately. Two other pirates also sounded angry and screaming outside of the mess room; I later found out that they had slapped around Capt. Ram and Parjeet on the bridge, suspecting foul play.

In a few minutes, Parjeet came down to the mess room escorted by a pirate, and called for Akbar Khan, the ship's electrician, known to all as 'Batti Sahab'. He was a funny guy with an almost circular goatee and a bald patch on his head. He hailed from Pakistan and was addicted to chewing tobacco. He would've been a great fit in a relaxed government job, but unfortunately, he was here with us. Batti Sahab had a bit of a belly and walked with his hands swinging loosely at his sides all the time. He was also a great storyteller, and when in the mood to narrate his tales, he always sat with one leg up and rubbed tobacco in his palms as he spoke.

Usually, when there is a power failure, the back-up generator for emergency light is supposed to kick in, but this time we remained enveloped in darkness. There was pin-drop silence among us. I was sitting next to Abdullah and we lit a cigarette each. I saw his old-school radium watch glowing in the dark. It showed 10.15, which would have been about when we took our first tea break on a normal working day. I just said 'teatime' to Abdullah, and he looked at his watch, smiled unexpectedly, and said, 'Forget tea breaks now.'

Thankfully, the power came back in some time. The oiler who had needed to pee was still holding it in. This was when Hamood finally accompanied him to the toilet. Upon their return, the pirate's eyes fell on half a loaf of bread that was on the table. He also saw jam, achaar (pickle) and ketchup. These things were very easily available on every table in the mess room and in the galley (the ship's kitchen). He approached the loaf in a hurry and tore off its plastic wrapper, crumbling some of the bread inside, and put it straight into his mouth without any toppings. Finding it dry, he opened the bottle of jam, tried to read what the label said and then tried the achaar bottle. He dipped his index finger in both bottles one by one, and then, using that very finger, spread the toppings on the bread. Then, he took a huge bite and chewed it wildly, crumbs falling everywhere and the jam and the achaar smeared on his face. He didn't know the achaar would burn all the way from mouth to ass, so when the sharp taste hit him, he choked and coughed and struggled to swallow, immediately asking for water.

It was evident he had seen food after a long time, and thus wanted to gulp down everything in sight. Being at sea for so long had taken its toll on him. For a moment, I felt pity, but immediately diverted my thoughts towards how the pirates would behave in the coming days when they saw more food and better things in our cabins.

Someone gave him a glass of water, and he gulped it down. Then there was more silence, before he play-acted drinking from a cup and uttered the word 'sha'. We understood he was asking for chai, and Muhammed was visibly restless about the prospect of making tea for the pirate. He started whining and complaining about having to work for them at gunpoint. He made the worst tea he had ever made—you could see by its consistency that it was mostly water and very little milk. When he handed the cup to the cadet pirate, he told Muhammed to take the first sip. I wondered what the fuck he was up to, before I realized he wanted to ensure it wasn't poisoned. Clever bastard, I thought.

Once he had determined its safety, the pirate took his first sip and made an ugly face, sticking his tongue out. Muhammed looked so frustrated that I thought he'd give the pirate a whack on the head, but he held himself back. Then, the cadet pirate made a new demand, holding up the tea cup and saying 'suka-suka'. What the hell did he want now? Nobody could understand till he began acting out what he wanted by stirring an imaginary spoon in the cup. We felt like we were caught in a game of charades before we realized that he wanted sugar.

He kept asking to add sugar to the cup till we thought the spoon would be able to stand vertically in it. Muhammed couldn't take it any more and blurted out, 'How much? You will die with so much sugar!' Abdullah intervened and calmed him down, reminding him that we were in this together.

This whole incident showed the cadet pirate who the two people in charge of the food were—Muhammed and our steward, Rashid.

By now, the engine had been temporarily repaired and boxed, and we were ready to move. Abdi came before us with a happy face, raised his hands and told us, 'We go Somalia.'

Abdullah spoke to him about the space crunch in the crew mess room, and asked if we could move to the officers' mess room, which could accommodate all of us. To my surprise, Abdi agreed.

Six hours into the hijacking, and every minute felt like an hour. We were constantly flitting between hope and doom.

Soon, it was lunchtime. Muhammed was still reluctant to cook, and we once again had to explain to him that refusal to cook was not an option in the situation. He, along with Rashid, went to the galley, but his unwillingness was apparent in the food he prepared. I imagine the worst jails in the world can't put out food as bad as what Muhammed made that day—boiled vegetable stew with rice. But we needed to fill our stomachs.

At this point, it came to our knowledge that the pirates were going through our cabins, looking for stuff they could take. My mind went through all the things that could be stolen—phone, laptop and wallet were definite write-offs. What would they do with the dirty clothes and used shoes? I was always fond of shoes, and was carrying four or five pairs, apart from working shoes, safety shoes and flip-flops. I was more saddened by the idea of losing my shoes than the 1,500 dollars I had in cash, which would have been enough for about two weeks of partying in Zanzibar. The loss of the laptop meant my study material, projects, as well as movie and TV collection would be gone. I've never been in the habit of clicking a lot of pictures, so had nothing of importance in that regard. The phone I had been using was a simple Nokia model with just calling and messaging services; the only eye-catching feature it had was a torch. There was no point carrying an expensive phone on board a ship those days because the internet was not accessible on the seas, nor were there many features or apps available like there are today. Once ashore, we would just make calls back home from the closest phone booth.

It was only a few days later that I saw one of the pirates wearing a pair of my shoes. I went on to find out that they had left me one pair each of sports shoes and slippers. The latter was already in tatters, and I had to stitch them up to be able to wear them.

My crewmates and I spoke about the PlayStation and the CDs we could lose. We had a FIFA league going on, which was likely to come to an end due to what legal experts would call 'force majeure'. Our lives were in danger, but to keep our minds diverted, we would talk about what games remained to be played in our FIFA league.

Even after Abdi's announcement about heading to Somalia, it took us about two hours to start sailing. But once we did, about eight hours into the hijacking, we came to know that there was now a warship following us at some distance.

Towards the evening, when Parjeet came to the mess to take his and Capt. Ram's dinner back to the bridge, he told us to be prepared at night, because he believed there could be some action. He told us that if anything happened, we should all just run to the engine room and hide. As stated before, by now, all crew members and cadets were in the officers' mess room. The Captain was made to stay on the bridge the entire time, and would be accompanied by either the Chief Officer or the Second Officer for six-hour stretches. When they weren't on duty, they would come down to the mess room to rest.

Third Officer Kuldeep had gone numb in the mess room. I remember him wearing a bright orange boiler suit; he would wrap a white bedsheet around his face and head like a shawl, and sit quietly in a corner like a saint who has taken a vow of silence.

The engine room was manned by Bada Sahab, the Chief Engineer, and Mir Balach, the Second Engineer, with two oilers on a rotating six-hour shift. Somehow, the Third Engineer, Ahmed Durrani, was the only person allowed to sleep in his cabin and walk around with no restrictions. God only knows what he told the pirates to get such privileges right from day one. We thought the pirates might have gone by his look—he kept a haji's beard—but by that logic, Bada Sahab looked more worthy of special privileges. Durrani always remained a mystery, as nobody interacted with him even prior to the hijack. He kept to himself and did not talk to anyone. He would just finish his duties and meals, and go back to his cabin.

Like Ali Baig, Bada Sahab and Batti Sahab, the Second and Third Engineers were also from Pakistan. Mir Balach was from Balochistan and Ahmed Durrani was a pathan from near the Pakistan–Afghanistan border. Their clans are usually known as 'hotheads', but our engineers weren't like that in any way. Balach was of medium height and slim build, wore his hair in a crew cut and kept a white stubble. He sported round spectacles and was extremely soft-spoken. Durrani, as mentioned before, had a haji's long beard and was ever smiling, though extremely reserved. Anytime anyone asked him anything, instead of replying, he would just smile and nod. He was over six feet tall and had big feet, which I had noticed when I spotted him in safety shoes during supply loading. On normal sailing days, he would either be in the engine room in his overalls or in the officers' mess during mealtimes in his pathani salwar-kameez.

After what Parjeet had told us, we braced ourselves for what we expected would be an action-packed night. We arranged all our shoes at the mess room door leading to the galley, to ensure that none of us tripped or twisted our ankles in case we had to rush to the engine room. Living on a ship had conditioned our minds to always think of safety first—it's very important to wear safety shoes and helmets in the closed machinery space of the engine room, as one can easily hurt themselves if precautions are not taken. I imagined that if we had to rush, we wouldn't have time to grab our shoes or anything, but I arranged mine with the others anyway. As it happened, it was the last time shoes were arranged in that area.

Every time someone would come back from their shift on the bridge or in the engine room, we would want the latest updates. We were told that the distance between the warship and us had now reduced to only six nautical miles, which finally told us why Parjeet believed there was a possibility of action. However, Baig wasn't sure the warship would take any chances to rescue us. I remember thinking why he was being so negative—didn't he want to go home? In my imagination, like in the movies, Navy SEALs would approach from a chopper and start shooting green lasers. Then, I remembered that a chopper would make too much noise, so if the SEALs wanted to do a discreet operation, they would use a small boat like the pirates' own skiff, and sneak aboard. Somewhere in the middle of these action-packed thoughts, I fell asleep.

If we knew we had a warship on our tail, the pirates knew it too, and must have made their own preparations. But they also knew that as long as they had guns and this many hostages, there wasn't much even a warship could do. I could imagine what I wanted, but the only true fact was that the pirates had all the power.

Those of us who managed to sleep that night went to bed with hope. After a whole day of negative thought spirals, we had something to look forward to. There was still a chance that we wouldn't have to live through months of uncertainty or exist in the worst of circumstances. Maybe our parents and loved ones would be praying that we returned alive and unharmed, and would have a sleepless night or two. But if the warship did attack and came out victorious, we would be home by then.

But this was optimistic, considering that our Zanzibari crew members, who knew this region best, only told us one thing since the pirates had taken control: 'Very dangerous people. They will not leave us, *baana* … very dangerous people.'

4

Settling with the Pirates

When we woke up the next morning, the walls of the mess room felt like they were staring at me. Nothing had changed. Although we opened our eyes with disappointment on the previous day as well, this morning, we felt even more dejected than we had the night before. Had anything happened during the night? Was there any contact with the warship? Did it do anything?

We were anxiously waiting for the Second Officer to come and collect breakfast for the bridge, so he could give us updates. When he arrived, all of us wanted to rush to him, but we couldn't do that because the pirates used to look at each of our movements suspiciously. So we kept our distance and he didn't look at us as he took his first meal of the day. This was when someone asked him in Hindi, 'Sir, *kya hua raat ko* (What happened at night)?'

We weren't allowed to whisper, as that made the pirates think that we were making some secret plans. So Parjeet casually said nothing had happened. He was careful to avoid words like warship, action and navy. The pirates didn't mind us talking in Hindi because it's not like they understood much English anyway. Choosing his words carefully, Parjeet told us that the '*doosra jahaaz* (the other ship)' had maintained its distance and there had been no activity or communication.

The warship continued to tail us in silence—it was keeping an eye but not taking any rescue action. If it had got too close, the pirates would've panicked; too far away, and we hostages would've panicked. In time, we figured the warship was just playing a psychological role in this situation, and that any action from it would make the pirates retaliate, putting innocent lives—our lives—at risk.

Since Capt. Ram was kept permanently on the bridge until we arrived in Somali territorial waters, he was secretly passing on messages to cadets and the crew through Parjeet and Baig. As the commanding officer, the Captain's most important task was to ensure the safety of the crew and the ship. His messages were generic—'make sure everybody is all right and not hurt in any way', 'remain calm and don't act out of rage or desperation', etc. He told us to listen quietly to what the pirates said. However, even these messages had to be passed on secretly as the pirates kept a close eye on us to ensure there was no revolt being planned.

I feel the Captain had a special corner for us cadets, because in us he saw his own teenage daughter. On board a ship, there's generally a very practical and professional atmosphere. But Capt. Ram knew that in most of our parents' minds, he was in charge of taking care of us, almost as if they had told him, '*Ab yeh aapke hawale*', like a guru to whom students are practically 'handed over'.

In the early days of the hijacking, Capt. Ram understood this very well. In fact, his care and concern extended not just to the cadets, but to the whole crew. He was trying to hold us together for whatever lay ahead.

It was definitely an uncertain future, and in these circumstances, moments of joy were rare and precious. The next day, 13 April, was the birthday of David John, a senior cadet who hailed from Kerala, and was known for his peculiar way of starting a conversation with a nasal 'aanh' sound. David was tall, skinny and long-legged. He was an expert at chess and playing cards.

During the day, we were all trying to keep his mood up by talking about what a celebration would be like during a normal sea passage, and others telling stories of what previous parties on board had been like. Then someone asked David what he would've done in his hometown. 'Aanh, hometown, you can't compare … Toddy and fish fry, all day party!' he said.

However, by evening, we ran out of conversation topics and I saw David grow quieter, settling in a corner and fishing out a photograph from his wallet. Around midnight, he stood up and walked to the pirate keeping watch at the door. This being only the third day since the hijacking, we had no clue how they would react to us approaching them, especially this guy at the door, who looked like someone who should be left alone. The pirates called him Aaden. He was tall and skinny, had a receding hairline and a long face that constantly wore an angry expression. Later on in our captivity, the way he chewed khat earned him the nickname 'Camel Face'.

When David walked up to him, we were all surprised. Then, he said, 'Aanh, hello brother, I want to go to my cabin for some time.'

Camel Face didn't understand a word, but the first thing he did was tighten his grip on his gun and use the other hand to sign his responses. 'What? Go sleep,' he managed to convey.

Abdullah was up by now; he turned to his side, used his hand as a headrest and joined us in observing what unfolded.

'Brother, I want to go cabin, my cabin, bring clothes,' David explained. He also signed going up and getting a pair of pants.

Camel Face repeated his actions, but then said, 'Ah, no.' Then he tried to ask David if he had no clothes down here.

David replied, 'Aanh, brother, no have.'

To our great surprise, Camel Face then said, 'Go, go, come.'

David ran to his cabin and returned with a pair of jeans and some T-shirts, but was holding them like he had wrapped something within. My first thought was cigarettes, but David didn't smoke. He looked at me with a grin and said, 'Bonge bhai, party!' The bugger had managed to hide beer cans inside the clothes, and all I could think about was how! At the start of the hijacking, when the pirates were going through every cabin, he had mentioned quietly to us that he had left a few beer cans out in the open, and I had joked to him that he had still not learnt to secure alcohol after the incident in Pakistan.

Naturally, we had thought about retrieving those cans then, but it was dangerous. The pirates would have most certainly been against alcohol, or at least that's what we thought. We also wanted to be sure that on the off chance that they weren't opposed to alcohol, they wouldn't get their hands on it, because who knows what they would end up doing to us in a drunken state!

But now, David had retrieved them. He wanted to celebrate his birthday, and he was daring to celebrate it with warm beer, right under the pirates' noses. After the success he found on his first trip, he mustered up the courage to walk up to Camel Face again and tell him he needed to fetch another pair of jeans. Again, to our surprise, the pirate let him go to the cabin, and David returned with more cans.

The next problem we needed to solve was how to hide the tell-tale hiss that escaped from a pressurized beer can when it was opened. We managed this through some synchronized coughing. We were risking our lives for warm beers, but we desperately needed that moment of joy.

Abdullah, lying on the centre table and observing us, chose to ignore the act at that moment, but the next morning, he reprimanded us for our carefree and reckless behaviour. I believe he also empathized with us and understood the significance of stealing such moments of happiness while an uncertain and potentially dangerous future lay ahead for all of us.

We had now completed three nights in transit with the pirates, and in the early hours of the fourth day, we finally dropped anchor off the coast of Somalia.

Immediately, a rush of people came on board the vessel in many different boats, with one common goal—pocket anything and everything they could. With each new boat that arrived, we saw our cabins torn apart afresh. I just sat there and watched, with all sorts of thoughts swirling in my head. Did my parents know this had happened, or were they still expecting my call from Zanzibar? Seeing them felt like a distant dream; when would I even get to talk to them next? I was desperate to hear their voices or get a glimpse of them. Tears were welling up in my eyes, but I was holding on to them really hard. Looking at so many desperate and hungry pirates, I wondered if this was a test life had thrown at me, in which every day was going to bring new challenges.

As the boats flitted in and out of our location, there was one important man who came on board. We went on to call him 'Tarjuman'; this wasn't his name, but a generic Arabic and Urdu word for spokesman or translator (as I found out later when I googled it). His English was way better than any pirate who had come on board till then, better even than some of our crew members'. He was of average height and had a big belly, wore black tights with a red vest and a red belt, and didn't wear slippers. I suspected this was his beachwear, because he knew he was going to get wet. His hair was short and his eyes had a yellowish tinge, like everyone else we had seen so far. But he stood out because he was the only pirate who didn't have a jawline—he had a double chin.

Tarjuman had to put in a lot of effort to climb up to the aft deck from his boat, which, along with the ladder, kept moving and swinging because of the waves. Huffing and puffing all the way up, he exclaimed, 'How did they catch your ship? It is so high!'

He was so drenched in sweat by the time he reached the deck that it seemed he had fallen into the water. Two men had to pull him up on to the deck.

Tarjuman took a seat at one of the bollards (short, thick steel posts welded on the deck to which ropes are secured) at the aft mooring station. Mooring stations are designated locations on the ship—forward, aft and midship—which are manned by the crew to secure or unsecure a ship when going or coming out of a quay or a port.

Parjeet was ordered to be present as the ship's officer to greet Tarjuman and take him to the bridge, along with Abdi, while their pirate cohorts received the tons of supplies coming in.

I was standing at the railing as the pirates loaded food for their own consumption. For a moment, it felt like any other port call, and I joked to Parjeet, 'Pilot duties here too.' When a ship is going to or coming from a port, a local pilot comes on board to guide it out of that area or channel. It is the duty of the Second Officer to receive and see off the pilot as a sign of respect. Parjeet smiled at my joke, but said nothing.

Coming back to Tarjuman, the guy was still catching his breath and wanted some water. Senior Cadet Zaheer fetched it for him. I didn't realize that I was staring at him until we made eye contact for a moment. Then I thought it was my turn to get kicked for crossing a line, like Senior Cadet Sandeep had been on the first day. But to my surprise,

Tarjuman smiled and asked, 'How are you?' I didn't have an answer to that.

Tarjuman then spoke to Capt. Ram and tried to assure him that he was our only friend among the Somalis. He said they would evaluate the cargo, call up the owner of the ship and place a demand for ransom. He assured the Captain that nobody from the crew would be harmed, and as long as we cooperated, we would be out of here in no time. He made it sound simple.

He also politely asked the Captain about the number of non-Muslims on board, and if by any chance there were any Christians or Jews. Abdi had asked the same question after the hijacking and the pirates had already been given a headcount of Muslims and non-Muslims on board. But we had told them there were no Christians or Jews or Americans on board, even though we did have two Christians, including Senior Cadet David. It was a good thing that Indian passports don't mention a person's religion, and David was thankful to whoever had thought of this. The other Christian on board was our welder Lucas, whom we called 'Luca Baba', but Abdullah was able to manage the situation without giving him away.

Our officers realized the importance of Tarjuman, so when he repeated the question, the Chief Engineer, Bada Sahab, tried to jump in to earn some brownie points. But Capt. Ram glared at him, so he kept quiet and sat down again.

The officers tried to explain to Tarjuman that the ship was actually in very bad shape—the best example being our engine, which hadn't been operational when the pirates had caught us. The pirates thought the ship was big and looked well maintained, so in their minds, all was hunky dory. But it wasn't—we had barely made eight knots en route to Somalia. Tarjuman, however, had only one thing to say, and he was right: 'Captain, you should have avoided this situation. Now, until the tax is paid, you can't leave. This is Somalia.'

When Parjeet narrated the details of this meeting at the bridge to the crew, a chill ran down my spine. But then came the good news—there would be a supply of cigarettes and tea leaves, so we didn't have to kill each other for access to those. With that, the Second Officer went back to the bridge.

A few hours since Tarjuman came on board, boats were still bringing in more pirates. But by this time, we had been split up again—the officers and cadets remained in the officers' mess room, while the others had been shifted to the crew mess room. The pirates agreed to this because now they had more manpower to keep an eye on us.

Suddenly, a gun went off—by now, I was able to make out the difference between its sound and that of a welding torch. The ship went into chaos, and everyone turned to look in every direction for a dead body. Those in the mess room, like me, couldn't get out to look, and were left wondering if we had been attacked by someone else, or if someone had finally come to rescue us. Was it someone from the crew who had revolted, or were the pirates fighting among themselves? The pirates monitoring us were also clueless, but super alert.

It turned out that one of the pirates climbing the ladder to get on board had lost his grip on his gun, and as it fell, he made a grab for it and fired it by mistake. News came in that he had managed to shoot himself. Abdi came rushing to Parjeet to ask about a doctor in our crew, and the location of the ship's hospital. He shouted, 'My soldier, my soldier! Bullet! Doctor! Doctor!'

Later, we found out that the bullet had barely touched the pirate. He had received a minor cut, but the other pirates lifted him on their shoulders as if he couldn't walk. They were acting as though he would die if a doctor didn't perform surgery on him. Later, when I saw the Hindi film *Gangs of Wasseypur*, there was a similar scene, in which Manoj Bajpayee overreacts to his son getting scraped during a shootout. That scene immediately reminded me of Abdi, and I couldn't stop laughing.

That night, Capt. Ram came down with Tarjuman to the officers' mess room to speak to us cadets. All of us who had been sitting down stood up as soon as they walked in. The Captain told Tarjuman that we cadets were future seafarers. Tarjuman told us in an encouraging tone, 'I am your friend. You go back very soon, finish your study and come back, work in Somalia.' We were all a little confused about the last part, but didn't have the courage to ask, 'Come back as what?'

Then Tarjuman left, assuring us that if there was any problem, we could reach out to him directly.

Capt. Ram came back to us and gave us some cigarettes, and then addressed us in a serious tone. 'Boys, this is going to be the toughest phase of your lives. You will be tested, and you will either give up or find out how strong you are.

Don't try to be a hero. It's paramount that we stand up for each other. It's the best thing you can do at the moment. Prepare yourself, mentally and physically. We are going to be here for a while. Stay strong,' he said, and then left.

Somehow, I felt as though he had been looking at me in particular, and remembered his 'spoilt brat' comment about me. But maybe that was just me overthinking.

We didn't realize the gravity of the situation at that time. Our stomachs were full and we didn't even have to work now—we had to just eat, chit-chat and sleep. Movies were playing, tea was flowing. For smokers, there was no shortage of cigarettes. The pirates hadn't yet touched us or tortured us in any way. Their tone was quite calm, reminding us again and again that they just wanted money. It was just a business transaction for them, and they didn't want to hurt us.

On the other hand, there was Muhammed the Chief Cook, who had already lost all hope. Many members of his family were in the shipping industry, and piracy had been present in Somalia for a while by then. He had told me during one of our tea sessions on the aft deck that he had a relative who had been on a hijacked ship and had been left in the sun on the deck for multiple hours every day as a form of torture.

Muhammed was someone who shouldered the responsibility for his entire family, so it was hard for me to relate to his state of mind. He had started reacting very negatively and agitatedly to everything. If anyone tried to have a conversation with him or asked him what he was cooking for the next meal, he would get very animated and flap his hands around, sometimes even while holding a ladle. He kept saying things like 'This is not a party going on here', and crib about how he had to cook for so many people. Soon, he even stopped responding to morning greetings. If at all he replied, he would just say, 'What good morning? What is good this morning?' Soon, people started avoiding any kind of conversation with him.

Then, the Chief Cook lost interest in cooking, and started serving boiled vegetables with a chicken sausage and some rice. Capt. Ram was furious and sent a message to Muhammed to prepare the meals properly, but he took it the wrong way and said, 'We are hijacked and you want to have a party!'

Capt. Ram did not react to this, but he soon called for the Bosun and told him somebody from the crew needed to be on standby to take over galley duties. The Captain also told Abdullah, 'Don't order anybody, ask who wants to volunteer. We are in unusual times and people are reacting differently.'

I loved Capt. Ram's approach. He was a true leader, using different means to get things done. That gave me and the other cadets motivation to play our parts when the time came.

I was too young to relate to how the Chief Cook, a man in his fifties, saw the situation. He didn't have the mindspace to think of his crewmates; he was paralysed by the thought of his daughters and sons. He wasn't being selfish, he just had different worries. Unlike most of us, he actually had to work while in captivity, and working with such low morale is an ordeal in any case, but his problems were compounded by the additional mouths of the pirates he had to feed.

We tried our best to be accommodative of Muhammed's behaviour. The Captain gave him helping hands, and he was told he didn't have to cook every day; that others could take over on some days. But his motivation kept dipping.

We initially thought it was fear. It was obvious that one would not be able to carry out normal chores in a situation like this. But there were a few other crew members who were doing their regular work as well. For example, the navigating officers always had to carry out their routine watchkeeping to ensure the ship remained in its anchored position and that there was no unusual shift of weight. All these things required hands on deck. Same for the engine room, where the team had to ensure no leakages or failure in the machinery that was still running.

A week had now gone by, and our life in captivity had begun in earnest. About thirty to thirty-five pirates were on board, watching us round the clock in two shifts. They were all over the ship, from the accommodation, going up to the fo'c'sle and monkey island. One of the pirates wanted to keep a lookout from the mast, but Capt. Ram made him understand that wasn't safe because of radar—if he spent too much time up there with the radar on, he wouldn't be able to become a father. God only knows how Capt. Ram was able to explain all that to the pirate, but he didn't go up there.

It was getting difficult for us to pass the time. We were taken for fresh air to the upper deck once a week initially. We felt like a herd of animals in a zoo. Every time we would pass a pirate, he would stare and hold his gun tighter. Whenever we got a chance to talk to a few of them who were comparatively polite or understood some English, we would only ask 'when ship go?', and they would say 'go one week'.

There was only one place on the ship that remained free of pirates, and that was the engine room. They were just too scared to go down there, and refused to allow any of the engineers to go either. At most, an oiler was allowed to make the rounds, but had to rush back up in ten to fifteen minutes.

Another week or so later, we were allowed to go to our cabins, one at a time, to grab the necessities from whatever was left. When I reached my cabin, it looked as if a storm had struck—everything was lying open, clothes were strewn about and there was no sign of any gadgets. I saw my wallet and grabbed it, hoping to find something inside, but it was empty and torn from the inside. The PlayStation CDs were lying on one side.

When we had been en route to anchoring in Somalia, I had been allowed to grab a few things, like a pair of jeans, a couple of T-shirts, boxers, shoes, a towel and toiletries. My stock of cigarettes and a Zippo lighter were also secure. This time, all I carried out with me was the pair of torn slippers.

We cadets had no work. The pirates kept the lights on through the night so they could keep an eye on us, which messed up our sleep cycle. At first, we slept at 0200 hours, then 0300 hours, and within a few days, we were sleeping after breakfast. We used to just sit and watch movies throughout the night and sleep through the day. We couldn't even go for a stroll on the deck to get some sunlight. Playing cards was a major pastime as well. We were lucky to be left with a TV and a DVD player, but some wise pirate had taken the DVD player's remote with him. Our CDs contained twelve movies each, and since there was no option to skip or fast-forward or rewind, we would press play in the morning, and by the time we woke up in the evening, it would be getting to the movie we wanted to watch.

The ship was anchored, but our lives were afloat, drifting towards nothingness. We had become like animals who were surviving for the sake of surviving. The only difference between us and the pirates was that we were not eating grass yet.

Capt. Ram understood our condition and was really concerned. He wanted to get us out of the mess room and wanted some change in our routine. One morning after breakfast, when we were all just about to go to sleep, Abdullah came in and asked us to get ready for deck cleaning. Baig had taken permission from the pirates for the deck to be cleaned that day, as the ship had become a mess, thanks to khat and food residue and whatever else one could think of. The plan was to spend the whole day cleaning and get tired so as to fall asleep at night and wake up the next morning, to try and bring our schedule back on track.

It did help. At the end of the day, we were so exhausted that we just crashed and fell asleep. The next morning, we got a dose from Capt. Ram and Chief Officer Baig to 'not fuck up' our schedule again.

To keep us active and awake during the day, we cadets spoke to Abdullah and got ourselves involved in fishing with the other crew. This became a major recreational activity. The Tanzanian crew were expert fishermen, who could just drop a line and catch one every time. We struggled in the beginning, hardly getting a catch for hours, but we got better with time. We would scatter some leftover rice in the water, and the fish would come rushing in for it and get caught in our waiting hooks. In one session, we would catch twenty-five to thirty small fish, and then discuss our day's catch and sizes. Catfish are known to eat garbage, and there's an abundance of that at the bottom of a stagnant ship. So we were surrounded by them and caught a lot of them. These were the cheap thrills of our hijacked life.

One by one, we began to run out of food supplies. Essential spices like turmeric and chilli powder were over in about three months; black pepper and salt didn't last much longer. Gradually, we got used to eating whatever was served up. When we did run out of salt, we started using salted butter to cook everything, because we had plenty of it in the cold storage room—one of the partners of the company was sending a lot of frozen products to Zanzibar.

Our flour got infested with insects. Someone suggested we take them all out, while someone else thought we should discard the whole thing. But we told ourselves that when we cooked the flour, the insects would die. So we kept using it, and to be honest, we never felt any awkward taste.

Thanks to the pirates' insistence on round-the-clock vigilance, the generator was running twenty-four hours a day. There were no restrictions on food either, and this worried Capt. Ram, who knew that ransom negotiations would not conclude overnight and that we were going to be there a long time. He raised the topic of rationing multiple times with

Abdi, and even others when he was absent. He told them that if we continued this way, we would run out of water, food and diesel for the generator sooner than calculated. But they didn't listen to him.

To the pirates' knowledge, the ship's cargo was at 70 per cent capacity, and some of the cargo was cars. So, to their minds, this meant we were worth a lot of ransom. However, the majority of the cargo was cement, which wasn't worth much. Although I have no way to know for sure, I heard it on the grapevine that the initial ransom demand was so high that even the biggest companies would try and bring it down. It was an unrealistic demand, even by pirate standards. They didn't realize that the cars were second-hand and not in the best condition. The design of the ship, with its big goal-post masts, was such that it looked imposing from a distance but was actually quite old and hence not worth much.

After getting turned down so many times by the others, Capt. Ram finally discussed the subject of rationing with Tarjuman. We now had very limited diesel, and once it was over, we would face serious problems. The engine was not in the best shape anyway, as it had been under repair when we had been hijacked, and with the pirates on board, it was fixed temporarily to be able to sail to Somalia. The ship needed proper maintenance and repairs, and hence, our dry-docking had been scheduled for when we arrived at our home port. We needed to ration the fuel. According to the Captain's calculations, the generator could run for a maximum of twelve hours per day. However, the pirates insisted they needed the generator for electricity and radar throughout the day, as they had to be ready for any kind of strike. An agitated Abdi said,

'We are at war with America. This is the Somali army, we are Somali soldiers and we have to protect the coast!'

Capt. Ram took a pause and looked at Tarjuman to say something, hoping the latter would talk some sense into Abdi, but he, too, was silent and, to Capt. Ram's surprise, agreed with Abdi. The Captain had to back off.

There was this one pirate who was really skinny, and used to wear a jacket that he had taken from someone in our crew. He was so tiny that the jacket looked like an abaya on him. He would walk with a slight tilt of the shoulder he hung his gun from. One day, he walked up to Abdullah, holding up his jacket and a paint can. He pointed at the back of his jacket and signalled something, and we realized he wanted to get something written on his jacket. We asked him what, and he replied, 'Coastguard Somalia.' We tried explaining to him that the paint can was for use on other surfaces, not cloth, but can one say no to a person holding an AK-47? Abdullah got the pirate's wish fulfilled.

Another of the pirates, named Omar, had damaged fingers, so we ended up nicknaming him 'Tunda'. Of all the pirates, we had the most interactions with him, because he often sat in our mess room, keeping an eye on us and watching movies. He must have been in his late forties or early fifties, his English was better than some of the others', and he was better behaved than them too. He told me that he had kids of a similar age to us cadets. I never dared to ask him how many.

In one of my conversations with Omar, he described the eastern coastline of Africa like the back of his hand, from Somalia to South Africa. This coastline was their 'hunting' ground. On the northern side, he went up to the Red Sea and even the Persian Gulf. According to him, Oman, Yemen and the UAE were also within reach. Finally, he said their goal was to catch hold of another American ship, and this time around, not repeat the mistake they had made with the *Maersk Alabama*, which had been hijacked in 2009.

The story of the *Maersk Alabama* was well known in shipping circles before the Hollywood movie *Captain Phillips*, starring Tom Hanks in the titular role, came out in 2013. We had all heard how the crew managed to get hold of one of the pirates in the engine room and took back control of the ship. The pirate clan was carrying a grudge about this, so it made sense why initially they were so curious to know if any Americans were on board.

My batchmate Bade, just before the hijacking, had gotten himself a crew cut that was common among the American army, and in fact, was fond of Americans and their culture. He had also spent a few months in America and the place fascinated him; plus, his skin was also quite fair, so Abdi and team always seemed to think we were hiding his actual nationality. Only when Tarjuman cross-checked his passport were they satisfied that Bade wasn't American.

In any case, the negotiations with the owner of the *RAK Afrikana* had begun. The pirates' ridiculously high initial demand slowed the process, as the owner surely must have countered with a low figure. This is the kind of cost that no business owner is prepared for, and who knows how the insurance process was going and how long that was going to take.

The pirates kept making their entrances and exits from the ship. When the first set of them went home, they called us on the ship to ask for our phone and laptop passwords. I gave mine for the Nokia phone and HP laptop in writing. This meant we were never going to see our gadgets again, and even the 1 per cent hope we had left was dashed.

For the first three months in Somali waters, the pirates' numbers on the ship would go up at night and reduce during the day. The numbers varied widely—there were days when twenty-five of them would be there at night, but just ten during the day. They seemed to have assumed that if there was ever going to be a rescue operation, it would take place at night. That's why they insisted on keeping all the lights on, and kept the radar running and properly manned round the clock. On the bridge, for half the night, they would keep asking the officer on watch if something was coming, or if they heard a noise, what it was. This wouldn't let Capt. Ram sleep, and he would often say, '*Behen chod sone bhi nahin dete* (Fuckers don't even let me sleep).'

But in time, we found out that whatever incidents occurred took place during the day, not at night.

At the beginning of our captivity, the pirates did whatever they could to keep us scared. Then we started asking them to let us go out, and things began to ease up. Soon, we could just tell them that we were going to the washroom, and could go to our rooms to fetch whatever was left there. They didn't create any obstacles.

One of the days, an interesting conversation happened between me and Omar. I went up to him and said, 'I want to go to the bathroom.'

'Okay,' he replied. But as I took a couple of steps, he followed me.

I asked if he needed to come along every time, to which he replied, 'Yes.' I tried to reason that it had been a while, and suggested, 'You can trust me now.' He said, 'I can't trust nobody—orders!'

'Where do you think I would go? Jump off the ship and swim to land?' I asked.

'I don't know, maybe,' he said.

'And invite my own death? I am not going anywhere,' I said.

'Now, you ask toilet alone. Tomorrow, your friend ask. Then want go outside alone, outside America—catch! Big problem. Me big problem,' he replied.

Omar's gaze was firm. But he thought more about what I said, and finally agreed. It felt like a victory to be able to go pee knowing no gunman was waiting outside the door. But it came as part of a trade-off, because Omar was having trouble sleeping and wanted a new mattress, and asked if I could fetch him one. I knew Third Officer Kuldeep had kept his mattress safely but was not sleeping on it, so I simply told Omar to get it from him. The comfort of the man with the gun was more important.

From here on, things started to relax further. Omar developed an easy equation with us and even played chess with us. Trust me, he was good. We would bet things like if any of us won, we would go home, and if he won, we would stay. The chessboard and pieces were fashioned by us from materials available on the ship itself—a wooden plank was coloured in black and white squares, and the pieces were improvised from items like empty AK-47 shells and LMG bullets. Foam filters from cigarette butts were used to identify the pawns, while other pieces were marked by different kinds of tape.

But moments such as these were just distractions, because soon after they were over and we were alone again, we'd get lost in thoughts of home, family and freedom.

Before us, one more ship was hijacked and anchored a few miles away in the same general area of the sea. From a distance, it looked like a chemical tanker, and there was a fishing trawler tied behind it. The pirates had mentioned both were Spanish, but we couldn't be sure if it was flying the Spanish flag or if the crew was Spanish, or the owners were sitting in Spain. In our case, we were an 'Indian' ship because the owner was Indian, regardless of the fact that he was sitting in the UAE, the shipping company was registered elsewhere and we had multiple nationalities on board, including Indian, Pakistani and Tanzanian.

I got to know that the trawler's ransom had already been paid, and it was in the process of leaving. It left around a week later, with absolutely no drama. We didn't see any action or any warships keeping an eye on it. One night it was there, the next morning it was gone. The rumour was the chemical tanker had been hijacked with the help of the trawler, and now it had gone out to 'hunt' again. With bigger boats as mother vessels, the pirates could cover greater distances to hunt; it was no longer just about the 'tax' for crossing Somali waters. But the trawler never came back. Turns out, the trawler was hijacked again, by a different group of pirates who had nothing to do with the people who had taken our ship.

The whole piracy operation was run like a business, complete with investments and challenges. The groups knew each other, but they functioned separately. Apparently, the trawler was used to hijack the chemical tanker because the owners couldn't pay the demanded ransom, and so an arrangement was found—reduced ransom in return for a successful hunt.

When we got to know of this, we just looked at each other, and without speaking, read each other's minds. How many hunts would it take for us to clear our 'dues', especially with the state our engine was in?

One of the first things that came to my mind after this was 'DTGH', which stood for 'days to go home'. Our pre-sea instructor introduced this concept to us, writing on the top right corner of our classroom board. As the date changed every day, this number would reduce.

But in our situation, we didn't know how long we were going to be here. And the end was indefinite.

In spite of the uncertainty, we always had hope of returning. When we chatted among ourselves, we said 'when' we go home, not 'if'. The problem with hope is that it tugs at your heart every waking minute. I slept and woke up with the same thought. That's what every single day in captivity was going to be like.

5

One Hundred Days

Life throws challenges at everyone in different forms. In a situation like the one we were in, one shouldn't shy away from seeking the support of people, or offering it to people in the same boat. And I mean 'same boat' figuratively as well as, in our case, literally.

The worst thing to do is give up, because if you do, it'll lead to other complications. If you decide not to offer support to your colleague, when you need it, no one will come to your help. A mental breakdown is far worse than a physical breakdown, because it could start without you even knowing it. For us, it could have started from missing our homes, our families, thoughts of isolation or being stuck at sea for the rest of our lives.

These thoughts did cross my mind all the time, but I wanted to keep myself distracted as much as I could. The only way was communicating with colleagues or even the pirates, reading or keeping our minds busy somehow. One just couldn't survive if left alone.

There's also a sense of loyalty and responsibility that one develops towards the group. This is an integral part of most people's upbringing. We were all in it together and tried to support each other in whatever way we could. However, when it comes to keeping one's stomach filled, everyone reacts differently.

The biggest example was the people who were keeping us hostage. They, too, were doing all this just to keep their stomachs full. Unfortunately, this malaise spread within our crew too, and a few of them betrayed the rest of us.

While all of us were sleeping in uncomfortable places in groups, Bada Sahab, the chief engineer, had become the second privileged to get free access to his cabin and sleep there. To us his excuse was his backache, because of which he had requested Tarjuman to let him do so. Thanks to his old age, senior position and maybe 'salaams' to the pirates, he got them to discuss things with him outside the knowledge of Capt. Ram. Bada Sahab was close to retirement; his glowing skin, white hair and long beard remained as well groomed as ever, never reflecting the situation we were in.

Bada Sahab smoked in a unique manner—he would make a fist and put the lit cigarette between the ring and the little fingers, then take deep drags from the thumb end of the fist. Whenever he would enter a room, the smell of his attar (traditional perfume) would precede him, indicating that he had just put it on. He was always dressed in clean clothes and carried a cup of tea and a full packet of cigarettes, and could be seen taking a stroll from his cabin to the aft deck or the bridge deck. He had the freedom to walk around anywhere and anytime.

Bada Sahab's body language was completely different from anyone else's when he spoke to the pirates—he was comfortable, as if they were old friends. He would stand with them on the bridge deck, or near his accommodation, or behind the galley on the aft deck, holding a cigarette in one hand and using the other to stroke his long, white beard.

Because of all this, resentment towards Bada Sahab crept in among the crew, but it had to be bottled up. This resentment wasn't because he was being favoured, but because he was sharing information to get preferential treatment. But now that it's been several years, when I look back, I don't feel anger against him. I have seen a lot more of the world and can empathize with Bada Sahab now—he was trying to survive, just like the rest of us. I was a fresh cadet, with very little responsibility in life—who knows what I would have done if I had been in his place now? It is easy to say 'I would've been a model team player', but the reality can be different. When the spotlight is on you, things can change. For example, when we ran out of cigarettes or milk powder, in our own way, we would go and mingle with the pirates. We would sit and talk sweetly to them to get what we needed. The difference was, we never sold any information or ratted out our colleagues.

Within months, the quality of our life in captivity started going down as resources began dwindling with every passing day. For the pirates it seemed like a festivity as they didn't bother about rationing. The first month was fine, but a ship can carry only limited supplies. We had already started noticing the physical changes in each other, given that we were seeing the same faces throughout the day, every day. While the pirates were gaining bellies, my trousers were getting looser with each passing week.

I started exercising to make up for the lack of movement in our lives; it was also good for sleep, just to tire out the body.

More members of the ship's crew started changing their looks too—someone grew his hair, while others just looked gaunt because of the weight they were losing. I didn't cut my hair even once since the hijacking, though the double chin had reduced considerably. One day, Abdullah saw me doing push-ups on the aft deck and came and sat next to me. He could not sit still; he would keep moving or shaking his legs when sitting and talking.

Holding a cup of tea in his hands, he said, 'You're no longer Bonge.'

As mentioned before, 'Bonge' was my nickname on the ship. It had been given to me by a former deck crew member from Zanzibar, who had signed off and gone home a few months after I had joined the crew in September 2009. 'Bonge' meant lumpy or chubby—at least I think so, because I haven't been able to find a proper meaning anywhere. I looked at Abdullah and replied, 'Ha ha, yes, thanks to Somalia.'

In the first few months, the pirates would get a live goat to the ship once a week, slaughter it and distribute the meat among everyone on board. But the frequency of this kept dropping, to the point where it would be many weeks before a goat was brought on board. As the food supplies on board dwindled, we reached a point where we would get only one piece of meat, a little rice and a slice of potato. Sometimes, we would get just one pav (bun), some gravy and a cup of black tea. If someone had milk powder left, he would use it, while the rest would just drink it like hot water. The pirates' tea leaves were of the lowest grade. They used to come in bags, like hay, and tasted weird. But beggars cannot be choosers.

Another task we had to do every few days was wash our clothes. Washing machines were a thing of the past for us, so this was where we used the famous Indian propensity for 'jugaad' (unconventional, cheap innovation), though the idea came from observing Abdullah and the other Zanzibari crew members even before the hijacking.

Once, I had been sitting near the railing when I saw a crew member tie one end of his sheet to a rope and just drop it in the sea. The waves hit the sheet forcefully, so it didn't even need soap for effective cleaning. Then, after about half an hour, he pulled the sheet back up, rinsed it with fresh water, and thanks to the heat on the deck, it dried up very quickly.

We followed the same process now, and though we didn't have the luxury of rinsing with fresh water, the process did save a lot of energy and effort. On the days the sea was a little rough, we would just tie ropes to the aft railings and let the clothes get washed by the waves. This was going pretty well, until one day Rashid, our steward, who was super lazy, tied a big lot of clothes to one rope, threw it in the water and went for a nap. By the time he came back, the knot had come undone and all his clothes were gone.

By now, it had become common practice for helicopters to come and observe from a distance what was happening on our ship. They would hover around, far enough to not be in anybody's firing range, maybe make some notes and then retreat. We had learnt to tune out that activity, as it didn't really change anything for us. The pirates would still fire some shots at the chopper, even though it was a futile exercise. They might have done it to try and scare the pilot or to send a message to other pirates that a chopper was around. The choppers would randomly show up either around us or near the chemical tanker and then move away, or sometimes head towards the coast and then disappear from view.

On one occasion, a helicopter came threateningly close to the ship. We had been in captivity for just over two months at this point, and the coast had only two ships anchored—ours and the chemical tanker. This was the time when everyone was just getting used to the chopper coming and going. Till then we still had some hope of release or at least something out of the usual every time we saw a chopper. A young pirate named Abshir was patrolling on the monkey island that time. It might have been his first ship—we had seen the other pirates order him around, asking him to fetch milk or sugar. All his bosses were off duty as it was daytime. He panicked and started spraying bullets at the chopper, and this time, apparently for the first time, the chopper returned fire. Abshir started shouting and alerting the others. The ones who were sleeping woke up in a second and rushed to the deck. We had no idea what was happening.

We were sitting on the bridge when all this started (by now the cadets and officers were spending their days on the bridge and nights in the officers' mess room), and suddenly heard a continuous spray of bullets. The bridge was right under the monkey island, which meant we were almost in the line of fire, and a bullet could easily penetrate the bulkhead and strike us. We instinctively covered our heads with our hands. The pirate from the monkey island rushed down and positioned himself with half his body on the bridge and the rest still outside on the bridge wing. He tried to look out and take cover alternately. That's when his gun got jammed. He was just a few metres from me, and I could see him clearly struggling with the gun. Even though the gun was mostly pointing upwards, he was pointing it in different directions as he tried to unjam it. He was sweating and panting profusely.

He then came on the bridge, locked the door behind him swiftly and told everyone to duck or lie down. He sat down near us to take cover. I could see his hands were shaking; he was clearly panicking. My worry was that this idiot was going to fire the gun inside the bridge by mistake. By the time he fixed his gun, the chopper had receded.

I was thoroughly confused about what had happened. Once it was all over and things had calmed down, I met Abdullah downstairs and asked him about it. He said, 'Nothing happened. The chopper came, and these guys started shitting bricks.'

I asked him why the chopper had come, to which he replied that by the look of things, the pilot was just getting bored and was looking for some action on a slow workday.

He said the 'return fire' from the chopper was only flares, and not even real bullets. 'You see what kind of people are keeping us hostage,' he said, almost pitying our captors.

It was always a joy to have a conversation with Abdullah, and it was especially so with this incident. He was an animated speaker who made all kinds of sounds and actions during his narrations, like when he mentioned a chopper, he made noises like the rotor blades. When he talked about guns firing, he made the corresponding sounds. I said, 'At one point, I thought we were going to get rescued.'

Abdullah started laughing and, before leaving, said, 'Pray, *baana*, pray for that day.'

Given that our Chief Cook was making terrible food, the pirates also realized they couldn't eat what he was serving up. So, after some time, they got a cook of their own, Abdullahi, but the catch was that he would only cook for them, not us. The new cook loved wearing bottom-hugging shorts and tight vests.

He used to make fluffy paranthas that looked delicious. They were made of maida (all-purpose flour), instead of atta (wheat flour), so they weren't the healthiest, but tasted great. By now, we were tired of eating fish. At that time, anything not cooked by Muhammed looked tempting. All of us looked at the pirates' food longingly, especially the paranthas.

One day, when we really couldn't hold ourselves in any more, Senior Cadet Samit Choudhary spoke to the pirates' cook and somehow convinced him to give him half a parantha. Samit was a proud and loud Jat from Haryana, who lived in Delhi.

He was about five-foot-six and slim-built, and our time in captivity had only made him skinnier. He was growing his hair and would walk around shaking his head every time his hair fell on his face. That day, Samit could not have been happier—it had been such a long time since any of us had had a parantha, and he'd had half a hot, fresh one, even though it was quite thick and was accompanied just by a cup of tea. I cannot really describe the kind of satisfaction I saw on his face.

That same evening, I went to the washroom and saw the pirates' cook coming out of the toilet. I waited for him to wash his hands with soap, but realized that the concept of washing hands after using the toilet was alien to him. He came out, rinsed his hands with the same water bottle he had taken to wash his rear, and headed straight to the kitchen to make some more paranthas. I didn't have it in me to tell Samit what I had seen. In the subsequent days, he would ask me if I wanted a parantha, but after what I had seen, my response was always 'not really'. In time, I made Samit privy to the pirate cook's toilet habits. That's when his craving for hot paranthas died.

We used to call the Somali cook 'Cookie'. After a month on board, he knew that we called Muhammed 'Chief Cook' and demanded an equally respectful name for himself, but everyone continued to call him Cookie. We used to ask him, 'Cookie, when ship go?' His limited English restricted our communication with him, so he would just point two fingers and go. We never knew whether he meant two days, two weeks, two months or two years.

His initial signals got us excited that maybe some movement was happening, especially as he carried himself as though he knew inside information from the bosses ashore. In any case, this was happening in the third month since we were hijacked, which was the average amount of time any vessel stayed, for example, the fishing trawler that had been allowed to leave.

As we neared the end of our third month, Cookie brought news that we were about to leave. He was visibly excited at the idea of our captivity getting over, and I couldn't really tell if it was his excitement that rubbed off on us or ours on him. We asked Omar if we were about to leave, and all he said was, 'Inshallah, yes! Inshallah, yes!'

Our hundredth day in captivity was not only a landmark in terms of numbers, but an important day as well, since Cookie told us we were going to be freed. I could see it on our Chief Cook's face as well that something great was about to happen, although he was usually very good at finding a reason to be morose.

Muhammed told everyone that he had woken up in the morning for his prayers, hoping for the best. 'Very early in the morning, even before the sun rose, I saw a line of car headlights on the shore. My first thought was that Cookie is right and we are going to be released,' he said, getting all of us excited. 'It like a festival, *baana*, with light, light, light everywhere. Too many lights, *baana*, too many lights.'

As soon as the generator was shut off at daybreak, I went to the bridge. There was a lot of movement happening on the ship.

I had never been in a hijacking before, let alone be freed from one, so I had no idea what to expect.

We could see a lot of boats moving around, so we optimistically waited for something good to happen. The boats were all moving between us and the chemical tanker. We then heard the noise of a small plane in the sky, but it wasn't visible from inside the bridge. We weren't allowed to go out, so we could only hear it. The plane made a few circles above us and the chemical tanker, and we kept trying to catch a glimpse of it through the bridge windows.

Just then, we saw orange smoke emanating from the water on the starboard side of the chemical tanker. There was a boat there, and its occupants had thrown a smoke float in the water as a signal to the plane. The plane then lowered its altitude and we could finally see the twin-engined craft.

We had no idea what was happening. As I was trying to figure things out, someone pointed and said, 'Look at the sky, above the smoke.' All of us started searching, but I couldn't see anything and got irritated. I wanted all of this to happen for me. Yes, I was being selfish, because I was desperate.

I could see the smoke disappearing and hear the sound of the plane getting fainter. I saw it drop something, and although I couldn't exactly make out what it was from this distance, I was sure whatever it was was the key to freedom. The dropped item splashed into the water and the boat went to pick it up, then went to the other side of the chemical tanker and disappeared.

That's when we finally realized that the movement had nothing to do with us, as we had been hoping. It was for the chemical tanker, whose ransom had been paid. Our entire crew sat and sulked.

That night, we spoke about what would happen next. As we looked at the chemical tanker, we noticed that it had its generator on, and was much better lit than usual. They had probably been rationing their fuel, but now that their ransom was paid, they could relax and plan ahead. On the outside, things looked the same—it was holding anchor at the same position. But the atmosphere inside the ship must have transformed. They must be excited and preparing to go home.

In the months before this, we sometimes used to stand at the bridge window and look at the other ship. We used to think there would be someone struggling on that ship as well, just like us, maybe even looking back at us. Sometimes the pirates would blow the horn of our ship three or four times, and the other ship would respond with the same gesture, making a joke out of it. We couldn't see actual human beings on the ship, but we felt as if we had built a camaraderie with the vessel itself. It was the only thing in our sight, apart from the water and the deserted shore.

The next morning, the chemical tanker was gone. We were alone at sea now, as far as our eyes could see. I was happy for that ship's occupants, who had managed to leave, but also sad that we were still there. Now, it was like being left alone in a quiet room—the silence was hitting me hard. It wasn't as though we had any communication with them, but now we were totally alone.

We discussed how far they must have gone already. Maybe Mombasa in Kenya, the closest port, or towards the Red Sea, or maybe the Persian Gulf. It gave us hope that maybe we would leave soon as well.

In reality, all it meant for us was that we would now stay longer. The pirates didn't have any other catch, so they were going to hold on to us, especially since it was monsoon in the Indian Ocean, which meant it would take them a while to catch another ship.

And so, our hundredth day in captivity was truly a turning point. It was the moment of truth. Until then, we were living under restrictions, but there was no real discomfort. The food was acceptable, electricity was being used for the majority of the day, and even with rationing, it wasn't that uncomfortable. For those of us who were unmarried and didn't have responsibilities, things were a little less stressful.

But now things changed. The attitude of the pirates took a U-turn and everything went south from there. Our negotiation was taking longer than the pirates were used to. It was nearing the end of July and the seas were getting rougher as the Indian Ocean monsoon was approaching its peak months. The waves and winds in these times are very strong. For the next few months, it's not easy for small boats to go far out at sea and be able to carry out pirate attacks. So in all probability, we would be the only ship on the Somali coast. The climate so far had been dry; it didn't rain a drop the whole time we were there until that point.

I wished I could be on the ship that had departed. Damn that chemical tanker!

6

Maa and Baba

The middle of the ocean can be a difficult place. When the weather is bad, waves crash against the ship, tossing it around. The concept of the shore seems like a peaceful haven; the heart longs for the quiet calm of being on solid, stable ground. This is how I felt in those days. Even though I may talk lightly about those times now, emotionally it was a difficult period.

Not a day went by when we didn't think about home, family and friends. At least once a week, one among us would just be intensely homesick and start to get all sorts of thoughts. Was everyone back home okay? Had they moved on from us? What life awaited us now? How long could we live this life of captivity? What worse did we still have to see or experience in life?

When I felt low, I would take a chair and sit outside on the bridge wing. I would keep my back to the sun, so that my face would be in the shade. I would just sit and watch the waves, letting my thoughts flow with them. The waves and the fresh breeze always helped me relax.

Among ourselves, we spoke about our families every now and then. I remember telling my batchmate SK about my childhood and my paternal grandmother. Being completely cut off from my family, I used to worry about my grandparents. How would they be handling this situation? At times I would fear the worst.

I told SK that my grandma would wake up at 4.30 a.m. without an alarm and begin household chores. She loved her schedule and was very particular about cleanliness. She never believed in the concept of machine-washing anything, be it clothes or utensils. And why should she, when her hands seemed to have the magic of cleaning? If you wanted something to look like it did when you bought it, you just needed to give it to her to wash.

After completing all her morning chores, she would cook and then take a bath. By 8 a.m., she would be done with everything and then walk to the temple, which was six or eight kilometres away. People heading to work would say they could tell the precise time just by seeing my grandma go about her day.

We all had similar stories about our parents, grandparents, friends and girlfriends. Every day, something new would come up, such as a funny encounter, which by the end would make us emotional because we missed them all so much and hoped to see them in good health whenever we went back.

It's very easy to locate any ship if it has kept its Automatic Identification System (AIS) on. Anyone online, from anywhere, can track the ship's position and passage whenever it is around a coast. I, too, had informed my parents about how to track our ship. My mother would've wanted to do this anyway, because she would try and track me even when I was living at home and went out with friends. Whenever I called them from a port, my parents would be excited and tell me, 'We saw your position when you arrived.' Soon, they were able to calculate how many days my ship would take to reach the next destination, plus/minus a few days, and start expecting a call.

Before the hijacking, it was the same scenario. If anything, there was more excitement, as one of the incoming junior cadets who was supposed to join the ship in Zanzibar was Dhruv, a family friend living right across from our home in Jaipur. Dhruv was at home with his parents, his bags packed, ready to fly out the next day, when he looked up the ship's position over dinner. My dear mother, like most Indian parents, packed some goodies and home-made snacks and sent them to Jaipur, so that Dhruv could deliver them to me on the ship.

Before turning in for the night, Dhruv and his parents saw the ship one last time on their monitor and spoke to my family, who wished the youngster a safe voyage and went to bed in peace. The next morning, the ship's position—which had been just off Seychelles—vanished from the AIS, but there was no immediate panic because it was not unusual. The location data was calculated via the closest land link, and at times the vessel would not be in range.

My parents and I used to speak every time the ship went in to port; I would either buy a local SIM card or find a phone booth. At the time, SMS was the only means of messaging, which wasn't very conducive to exchanges with family. Instead, I would update them fully about how I was, where I was and where the ship was headed next. They would share family news, like who was getting married or who had had a child.

When I had called them from Seychelles, I had told them we would reach Zanzibar in five or six days. I had a Zanzibar SIM from my previous trip there, when I had joined the ship, so I told them I would call them.

The news about the hijacking was broken to my father a day after it happened—the ship's owner emailed him that evening. Those days, even the media didn't cover such incidents so quickly and in detail, so the word hadn't yet got out to anyone except the company that owned the *RAK Afrikana*.

My father didn't know how to give my mother this news. Instead, he replied to the owner's email, asking for more details. But he wasn't satisfied with the response, as the company itself didn't have much information then. So, he decided to get on a call with the owner and tried to get as much information as possible before breaking the news to my mother. The new cadets' travel plans had been cancelled by then, but no reasons were given.

My dad worked with a leading chain of colleges that had centres in Indian and the Middle East, and he had recently been posted in Ranchi from Dubai at that time. The next day, out of the blue, he came back home at lunchtime. My mother found it unusual and knew immediately that something was wrong. Normally, she would have asked why he was home early, but maybe she read his expression and instead asked, 'Is everything okay?'

Her first thought was that something had happened to my paternal grandmother, so she asked about her well-being. Then she thought my dad had had some trouble at work. Bad news related to me was nowhere on her mind.

My father just said, 'Arjun.' This was my nickname at home, given to me by my elder brother, who was fond of the third Pandava brother in the Mahabharata. The earth slipped from under my mother's feet.

'*Zinda toh hai na* (He's alive, right)?' was all she could ask.

My father went silent for a minute, and tears starting rolling down my mother's expressionless face. He told her about the email he had received from the ship's owner in Dubai and conveyed everything he knew about the hijacking. He told her we were still en route and it would take four or five days to reach Somalia. My mother cried harder; the thought of four or five days in these circumstances felt unbelievably long to her. My father tried to comfort her, saying the company was trying to resolve the situation to the best of their abilities. He barely had any information other than that, which made it even tougher.

Mom and Dad got on the phone with Mom's youngest brother (my mama, or uncle), who lived in Muscat, Oman, only a few hours' drive from Dubai. He volunteered to drive to Dubai immediately and meet the owner. Both Mama and my elder brother Pramit had strong, dominating personalities; back in the day, they were the two people I always went to when things went awry for me.

In tough times, it's comforting to hear stories of other people having gone through the same ordeal, but my parents couldn't find any such stories. There were only horror stories on the internet about Somali pirates. For two or three days, my parents stayed quiet, still processing everything that was happening. Their only confidant was Mama.

Gradually, my parents started gathering more information. They got to know that it usually took two to three months to free a hijacked ship, and they held on to that hope. My mother's heart sank—initially, the thought of four or five days felt so long, and now, here they were, talking about two or three months. It was unbearable for her. She didn't know at the time that God was testing our whole family's strength and that two or three months were just a fraction of the time I would spend in captivity.

Mama arrived in Dubai and met Capt. Aarya, a sailor himself with a massive career at sea who had now become the owner of *RAK Afrikana*, a nice and cordial man originally from Jammu, who must have been in his fifties at the time. Capt. Aarya's demeanour was respectful but also business-like. My uncle was furious and confronted him, saying the company was not providing adequate information. The owner met his aggressive questions with polite responses, which frustrated Mama even more, because at such times, what people want are immediate answers and results, and nobody cares about politeness. At the same time Pramit was also trying to reach Capt. Aarya over the phone and getting furious with the replies.

Much later, we all understood that it wasn't really the owner's fault; the company, too, was at the mercy of the pirates. If the pirates didn't answer the calls, they couldn't get information. The owner couldn't share sensitive information or any kind of negotiation strategy with families, and moreover, any kind of media coverage or publicity would work in the pirates' favour, because they would feel that their captives were important people, and hence, would increase their demands or make negotiations difficult. But which family would listen to all this when their husband, brother or son was being held at gunpoint?

The first week after the hijacking was very tough on my mother. She barely slept and experienced a high level of anxiety. Every morning she would ask my dad: '*Koi khabar? Kuchh aaya* (Any news? Anything)?' He would have nothing to share.

They tried to talk to people in the industry to gather whatever information they could. I still don't know how true it is, but they were told that the US hostage negotiation policy is strictly opposed to paying ransoms, and this stance was being emulated by many other countries. My parents were told that if the Indian government paid up, the pirates would start targeting Indians.

In 2010, the situation was quite unlike some recent brave evacuations, where the Indian government had ensured its nationals returned home safely. The company we were working for was not even registered in India, and on top of that, there were multiple nationalities on board. All this further complicated matters.

Capt. Aarya was also trying to figure things out. The whole negotiation depended on the insurance company: What did it think was the value of the cargo? How much did it believe every human life was worth? How does one calculate the worth of a life?

For some reason, he appointed a point-man for the negotiation, and told the hijackers that he was a third-party negotiator. This was our training superintendent, Capt. Nair, who was in his mid-sixties, from what I remember. He was not very tall, but was fit and active. He had a moustache and always smoked with his left hand because he didn't want his right to smell when he shook hands with someone. Capt. Nair held an extra master certification, which meant that upon becoming a captain, he had to appear for another set of exams to get this dual certification, which was not very common. He was senior to Capt. Ram and Capt. Aarya, and in his prime had sailed with major oil companies and was also the captain of the biggest oil tankers back in the day.

I still remember his first day as our training superintendent. He took one look at our shoes and made us spend an hour polishing them. For him everything had to be spic and span. He used to say, 'A man should always be ready in a way that he can go on a date any time.' He had joined our training batch a few months before the end of our semester, so we didn't get to spend a lot of time with him, but did develop a close bond with him. His knowledge and experience was immense, and he was a true industry veteran and role model.

When people feel helpless, they do whatever they can to get out of it. It is natural to turn to God, but God doesn't answer questions. Then come people who recommend godmen ('babas' or sadhus), who can answer questions. So my parents, as well as the parents of my colleagues on board our hijacked ship, turned to a slew of babas for guidance, each of whom demanded different kinds of dakshina (donation) from them. Pramit, my elder brother, was against the idea of my parents visiting babas, knowing that people will always try to take advantage of those in vulnerable positions.

The first baba my parents went to said he had had a vision where he could see a child sitting near an ocean in a white vest and blue jeans, surrounded by dark-complexioned men. He told my parents to organize a pooja and listed out all the things required for it. He told them this would need a special kind of wood, which was not easily available, and was thus expensive. My parents complied, but needless to say, it was unsuccessful.

Another baba asked them to donate many kilos of ghee, but didn't want them to buy the ghee themselves—he wanted the cash with which he would 'buy the ghee himself'. A batchmate's father, meanwhile, was told his son would return if he stopped cutting his hair.

Since our Indian crew hailed from many different states, I expect that babas' revenues shot up all across the country that year.

Then, one of my father's colleagues told him about a baba in Jaipur, who sounded so fishy that even my parents at the height of their desperation didn't want to meet him. However, my father's colleague insisted so much that they had to go. The place reeked of shiftiness from the entrance itself. The ceiling was low, to make sure everyone had to bow their heads to enter. It was convenient for the baba, though, as he was short. There were people giving leg massages to the baba; the whole place felt like a don's den. Even my parents could tell that the people here were being brainwashed.

The baba heard the whole situation and said my time in captivity was almost over. He said my parents would need to arrange a maha yagya (grand prayer and fire sacrifice), which would cost just one lakh rupees, and I would be home the next day. By now, my parents had come across so many babas that they knew it was all talk and no action; that no miracle would happen overnight. But they still had hope, so they clung to it and went ahead with the expensive pooja.

When the babas failed, my parents took to praying and fasting relentlessly to see if God could be swayed. They went to temple after temple and sat there praying for my long life. In tough times, one falls back on faith, not people, and faith was all they were holding on to. Prayers were also a pillar of support to my extended family.

On some days, my mother would just go silent, and tears would flow without her knowledge. She would just sit and go deep into her memories of me. My dad would try to comfort her, and to lighten things up with a bit of humour, would tell her to note down the date and time, so that when I returned, they would ask me if I felt something at the same moment.

Every person they spoke to offered a different answer—someone said fifteen days, another said three months. It was difficult for my mother to live on without getting any information about me. She even started to lose faith in her prayers, as they didn't seem to be working.

Throughout my absence, my parents decided not to tell my grandparents, who were in their eighties, and my uncle Gandhi Baba, who was a heart patient, about the hijacking. Gandhi Baba was our neighbour in Pilani, India, when I stayed there back in early 1990. I was in kindergarten then, and I practically lived in his arms and grew up around him. He was an electrical engineer and his love for fixing things, with me sitting down on a small chair across from him, eating watermelon or mango from a steel plate, are some stories that his family and I still talk about. I feel it was the best decision not to tell him or my grandparents. Whenever they would ask about me, my parents would suppress their own emotions and lie that they had just spoken to me and everything was fine.

After my return, my mother told me she had remembered a story she had read when she was a little girl, about a child who went to a local fair with his parents. The child wanted to go for a joyride, but his parents said no. Then, he asked for sweets, but his parents turned down that request too. Then, he asked for balloons, but his parents once again refused. Suddenly, owing to the crowd, the father lost his grip on the child, and he got lost. A stranger found him crying, and to calm him down, took him for a joyride, bought him a balloon and some sweets. But the child kept crying because now, he only wanted his mother and father. All that he had wanted earlier lost meaning.

This is how my parents felt—everything they had wanted till now had lost importance. The only thing left for them was to see their son return. They fought a lot with the ship's owner; my mother was never satisfied with Capt. Aarya's efforts.

In these months of duress, the families of all the Indians on board the ship grew quite close to each other, speaking on the phone and exchanging a lot of emails. They consoled each other, even though all of them were equally clueless about when this ordeal would end. If anybody got any information, it was immediately circulated among the others. Several times, news came that all of us would be released in a week, but they were left disappointed every time.

On one stressful day, news broke about a ship whose crew had been released. The crew, speaking to the media, shared stories of torture—they were badly beaten up and ill-treated. There was a phone recording of one of the captive crew members with his family, in which he was talking about the torture, and pleaded with the government to do something. The media went to town with this story, and it even became a talking point in Parliament. But imagine how it would have felt to my parents as well as to those of my colleagues.

They feared it was inevitable that similar things would be happening to their sons in Somalia.

My mother wrote letters to Capt. Aarya very frequently, and most of them were quite blunt. He would also respond to her immediately. In spite of her bluntness, whenever they came face to face, the ship's owner was always humble and cordial. He didn't complain about the harsh language in the letters, nor did he say that the blame was unfair. He understood a mother's heart, and that she had written everything she had out of desperation to see her son. The other families also vented their frustration in several meetings, but Capt. Aarya was always calm and composed. However, the families felt frustrated with the lack of any progress being made. The owner was their only source of news, and he assured them that everyone was alive and okay. But my mother wouldn't hold back, and narrated to him the stories she had heard about things that happened on hijacked ships, and the shady things ship owners would do for money.

In all, my parents made three trips back to Dubai to meet Capt. Aarya. But their efforts didn't speed up anything. He, in turn, told my parents not to research too much, but they kept reading all they could about ships getting hijacked and released. There were ships hijacked after ours, but they were released way before ours. This added fuel to the fire.

What our families didn't know was that the delay in releasing our ship wasn't just about the ransom money. There were practical challenges with the negotiation.

Midway through the negotiation, Tarjuman disappeared for three or four months, because his mother was apparently very sick. This happened again and again, and the outcome was that the negotiation came to a standstill.

The worst happened when, during this time, our superintendent and the negotiator on behalf of the company, Captain Nair, died in Dubai. We received the news via a phone call from Tarjuman to one of the pirates on board, and we cadets, in particular, were heartbroken. The owner, while mourning the superintendent's death, immediately hired a company from the UK to carry forward the negotiation.

The actual reality of the negotiation was different. As I mentioned in the previous chapter, all this was happening during peak monsoon season in the Indian Ocean, and the coast where we were anchored had only one ship after the chemical tanker was released. The pirates did not want to leave the coast empty, so we were stuck.

Between all this, on board the ship, my batchmate Bade found a newspaper cutting from the UAE. Whenever we went to any country to load or discharge cargo, Capt. Ram had instructions to the clearing agent to bring in the newspaper daily. In the port calls in Sharjah, a newspaper was delivered onboard which had an article about the graduation ceremony at the university where my father was the dean, and he was visible right in the centre of the photograph, surrounded by students and faculty members. Bade joked, 'If the pirates get hold of this and realize your dad is in the papers, they will target you. And if you don't share your cigarettes with me, I'll give it to them.'

We laughed about it, but at night, I took out that cutting and looked at it before going to bed. Before I knew it, I had tears in my eyes. I couldn't control them and I didn't want to.

I took the cutting and kept it under my headrest, turned to the side and cried the whole night, thinking about my parents.

7

The Pirate Code

Over our months in captivity, my mind started wondering about the bigger questions behind such operations. For example, being forced to look at the pirates round the clock, I couldn't help but wonder how they came to be in this profession. What kind of society did they belong to? And most importantly, why were Somalis getting pushed into piracy? That was something I asked myself again and again. Gradually, I learnt the answers to some of these questions, while most others remained unanswered.

Supplies were delivered to our ship regularly—sugar, powdered milk, pulses, potatoes, onions, rice, flour, spaghetti, tea leaves, live goats to be slaughtered for meat, cigarettes, khat, etc. Every evening, we were all scattered across the ship minding our own business. By now people could come out on the bridge wing and inform the pirate on the monkey island that they would like to sit out in the fresh air for a bit. The Zanzibari crew could move around from their mess room to the galley until the aft deck, where they would fish. By evening someone or the other would spot the supplies coming in and alert everyone else with cries of 'Boat! Boat!'. Then we would all run towards the edge, pirates and ship crew alike, behaving like drought-stricken villagers celebrating the first drop of rain.

Most of the supplies were delivered once in a few days, but fuel for the generator came every day. The generator needed to be run for a few hours in order for one full meal to be prepared for the day, and to fill enough freshwater from the watermaker. We were fortunate that throughout our captivity, we did not face any acute shortage of potable water, because we had a watermaker—which desalinates seawater—as our saviour. Under normal circumstances, this would not be the preferred option for drinking water and would only be used in emergencies, but as Second Officer Parjeet had remarked to us, we left behind 'normal days' at the last port. Now, the watermaker produced potable water for only the short duration that the generator ran, and that kept us going.

The fuel came in twenty-litre plastic jerry cans, and the laborious task of lifting them from the boat to the ship was assigned to the hostages—more specifically, to the lowest in the ship's hierarchy, the cadets. Every time the boat arrived, we ran to the edge with long ropes, lowered them to the boat below and pulled the fuel jerry cans up. Once that was done, we gave the fuel to Batti Sahab (the electrician) on the deck, and he turned the generator on. Then we all ran to fill our own water from the watermaker in plastic cans, bottles, containers, jerry cans, whatever we could use as storage until the next day. To us hostages, who had been living without adequate electricity and water, the arrival of the boat with the fuel symbolized survival.

Naturally, under such circumstances, there were disputes over the supplies. One evening, I was sitting on the bridge and sipping tea, which we had prepared on a makeshift firepit (like the angeethi in north India), when I heard someone yelling. I got up, reached the edge of the bridge, and saw the pirates' storekeeper, who was also called Mohammed, and another pirate shouting at each other. They were arguing about something we couldn't understand. After a while, both of them picked up their guns, and though they didn't point them at each other, their rage was frightening.

As our stay got prolonged for the variety of reasons mentioned before, the pirates' supplies were also becoming scarce. This argument had been about khat, which was a caffeine-like necessity for them to keep awake whenever they were on duty. In the latest supplies, one of them had received an extra bunch of khat. Usually, they would receive a new batch once a week, along with other necessities, and they were supposed to use it wisely. But given the conditions we were in, most of them ran out of khat before the next supply came in.

Their frequent quarrels over the supplies made us think about their situation—we all wondered how poor they would have to be to fight over such petty issues. There were also other characteristics that displayed their poverty, such as the fact that we never saw any of them wearing clean or new clothes. Even when they came back after spending time away from the ship, their clothes were unclean, torn, and their appearance remained unkempt. Also, they always went through our stuff and looked for things they could take away. I can only imagine that they were snatching these things from us and giving them to their children back home as gifts.

Moreover, they showed complete disregard for any acceptable levels of hygiene and cleanliness. When they ate their food, they sat on the floor. While this could still be considered normal, what we found repulsive was the condition of the area where they sat and consumed food. The place was one of the filthiest spots on the ship—it was not appropriate even for sitting, let alone eating. Under normal circumstances, that area would be cleaned with a strong disinfectant before anybody could even think of sitting there. They, however, happily consumed khat, smoked and left behind cigarette butts strewn in the area. They even spat in and around the area, and then ended up eating and sleeping there.

There was one particular image of one of the pirates' activities that left a long-lasting impression on my mind: how they made and ate spaghetti. It was understandable that the spaghetti wasn't the best-cooked, given the circumstances, but they merely boiled it and put loads of sugar in it. But every time they ate it with their unclean hands, it appeared as if they were eating the last meal of their lives, or their first one in ages. The visual has forever turned my appetite off spaghetti.

In time, as supplies ran lower and lower, the pirates started getting more frustrated, and not many of them wanted to come back to our ship. They admitted that negotiations with other ships happened much more quickly than this one. But looking at their operations and thinking about it, I was curious that if they were making so much money off piracy, why hadn't their standard of living improved? They might have been exaggerating the amount they had made off other ships, but even assuming that, where was all of it going? Looking at them and the way they appeared and behaved, it certainly didn't seem as though the money had trickled down to them and given them any level of financial well-being.

At times, to pass the hours, the pirates or one of us captives would start a conversation about life back home. One particular conversation gave us some more clues about their philosophy of life.

That evening, the generator hadn't been turned on and thus all of us were outside on the deck. Suddenly, we saw a helicopter hovering over the water, and a boat going full speed ahead towards it. Owing to the distance, we couldn't make out exactly how far they were from each other, but then, suddenly, the boat went up in flames and a cloud of smoke billowed out of the water.

Abdi was on board that evening, and he jumped towards Parjeet to grab his binoculars. I was a few steps behind both of them on the bridge, looking at the burning boat. Abdi ran towards the radio, changed the station and started speaking fast in his native language. But he didn't get a response. He again looked through the binoculars at the boat and went silent for a moment. He looked at Parjeet and said it was possibly his brother's boat, as he was supposed to go 'hunting' to catch a mother ship, from which his team would go further into the ocean to catch a cargo ship like ours. He closed his eyes for a moment, said a prayer internally, and that was that.

That made me feel even worse. If this was true, and his brother had just died in a fireball, he seemed very indifferent. There were absolutely no signs of pain, suffering, sadness or remorse in his voice when he started a conversation with his subordinates again. When Parjeet asked Abdi if he would be going home, he replied, 'Aah, no need', and something about how his brother had two wives and many children. That was his only reaction to what was a family tragedy.

I immediately thought that, God forbid, if this were to happen to any of us during normal passage, it would be so difficult to pass the time until we reached the next port, even if we were just going to sign off and head home to be with our families. And here he was, laughing and smiling, not even bothering to check over a phone call if his brother had even been on the burning boat.

There was only one further thing Abdi said about it. 'This is pirate life.'

Another such conversation I had was with the pirates' storekeeper Mohammed, who had replaced 'Cookie' on board and was now also the new cook for the pirates. He asked me about the currency used in India and I said it was the rupee. It amused him that Indians accepted only one currency, and he added with pride that on the streets of Somalia, all the currencies of the world could be used to trade, shop and do business.

He then asked if I had any Indian rupees on me, and I replied, 'The only thing your friends have left me with is what I am wearing.' And we both laughed.

All these conversations made me realize the pirates' outlook on life—they were devoid of any sense of responsibility that the rest of us feel towards our family and children. We still knew nothing about how they became pirates in the first place. Of course, we had some general knowledge about how radical organizations operate around the world, providing people rigorous training in combat, communication, arms and ammunition, etc. But being a pirate was more of a freelance job; most of them volunteered for it at a young age, and even migrated to it from white-collar jobs.

Mohammed, for instance, had worked for the Somali government, but was only given food in exchange, not a salary. After quitting his government job, he joined a very active radical organization, where the incentives were better, as along with food, he was also given cigarettes and, as he put it, 'small money'. But his monetary aspirations were higher. Also, they did not give him khat as it was considered haram (forbidden). After that, he started working in a neighbouring country as the captain of a speedboat. This is where he proved his ability to manoeuvre a boat well in the rough seas, and thereafter, it wasn't tough for him to get picked up for hijacking operations. He preferred being a pirate because he got 'food, cigarettes, money and khat … And now, I have three wives to enjoy.'

Every day, before the generator was turned on, we used to spend our day outside on the bridge. It had become a habit and we had put a wooden bench on the bridge wing and brought in some chairs. We would just put our legs up on the railing, taking shelter from the sun, and look at the calm, quiet sea. This had become a habit among us. One day, most of the crew members, including Bada Sahab and Second Engineer Mir Balach, were around.

The pirate we called 'Jafar', whom I have mentioned earlier as the guy who had put a gun to my head, was on the monkey island with his cigarette, gun and khat, keeping a vigilant lookout. He was wearing a lungi and a vest, and had wrapped a large piece of cloth resembling a bedsheet around him. When he saw me looking at him, he came down to where I was sitting. He used to keep his cigarettes and lighter tucked into the fold of his lungi around the waist, and now he took them out and lit one. Then, he offered me one too. It was a strange moment—captor and captive having a conversation over a smoke, like regular people.

I had asked many of them how people became pirates, and now I asked Jafar the same question. He was the oldest of the current lot, and I had always kept my distance from him after the sounding incident. But now, over the cigarette, I mustered up the courage to ask him the question, avoiding the word 'pirate', which they didn't think they were—to their minds, they were the Somali coast guard.

In reply, Jafar pointed to the shore, and I'm paraphrasing what I understood of his response. 'You see the land there?

There are many people spread across the coastline just waiting for a single meal a day. They all have their weapons, as guns are easier to get than toys. One boat that goes out to sea can accommodate maybe six to eight Somalis, but they all want to go on that boat, because they know with one catch, their life is secured. For all of them, it's one opportunity that they need.'

The conversation continued, and I learnt that out of all the people scattered around the coast, the ones who own boats offer their services to whoever comes asking. The boat owners then start looking for a crew and choose people mostly based on friendships, though merit has some weightage as well. This merit, naturally, is gauged from previous hijacking experience and skill sets. One needs only three skills to become a pirate, or 'Somali coast guard'—manoeuvring a boat, shooting a gun and swimming. I didn't understand why swimming, because it's not like they could swim back ashore from where they operated. But I didn't press it, because who wants to reason with them?

Jafar mentioned that after taking control of a ship, they were required to inform the people higher up the food chain. In the case of our ship, it was reported to a bigger and more prominent radical organization operating in the area, although we never saw them or heard them calling on the phone. Maybe we were just not informed when they came, as it didn't matter to us; they could've been any of the pirates that came and went. They might have communicated through VHF radio or used their cellular phones, but we were never privy to that information. As far as we knew, the pirates on our ship were operating independently. However, it did become clear to us that there were two distinct entities the pirates were afraid of—on land the radical organization, and out at sea the patrolling warships of various countries.

Years later, when I watched the film *Captain Phillips* about the *Maersk Alabama* hijacking, I could connect what I learnt in captivity to what they showed in the movie. The pirate recruitment process in the movie was just as I had imagined it to be.

I also learnt from Jafar that catching a ship was a matter of pride and achievement—the bigger the ship, the greater rewards they were bestowed with. The most difficult task was to hijack container ships. Anybody who caught an American vessel or crew was rewarded most handsomely, especially after the *Maersk Alabama* incident. As a matter of fact, from a tactical point of view, hijacking our ship had not been an easy task either. Nevertheless, here we were.

The political and social instability of Somalia played an important role in their life choices. After everything that I had learnt about the pirates, I could make the connection too.

Somalia is one of the most violent parts of the world. Since the 1960s, the country has never had political stability. A raging civil war has ravaged the country and left no scope for economic development. Most of the inhabitants are extremely poor, with no opportunities for peace and prosperity. If the people had the opportunity, they would have made better choices with their natural sailing skills, but unfortunately, making a living by capturing a merchant ship using guns made more sense to them than anything else in their given situation.

Apart from their country's instability, Somalis were hampered by the fact that fish was the only commodity they could trade. But lately, other countries—some which were far off from the Horn of Africa—had started fishing in their waters, and this had not gone down well with the Somalis. The others would use advanced technology, while the Somalis lagged behind because of their inferior and outdated technology and infrastructure. This, primarily, had been the cause behind the rise of piracy—they found it lucrative to hijack such boats and demand ransom, so as to be able to make money even as their fishing grounds were taken over by other countries. From smaller boats they started going further away from Somali waters and started hijacking bigger ships for higher ransoms.

From what the pirates were saying to us, it seemed they had been getting paid millions of dollars from hijacking other ships. But that didn't square with the circumstances of the people doing the legwork. So, where was all the money going? Did this mean there were bigger players involved? Maybe a higher political power squeezing these low-level pirates out of all their earnings? If yes, who were these powers? Who was holding all the cards in this game of life and death? Who was benefiting from piracy?

Our senior officers told us that piracy in and around Somalia had been going on for years, and speculation was out in the open that governments and other international agencies were benefiting from it too, because where there was piracy, there were countermeasures.

Ever since the Horn of Africa became a stronghold of pirates, war risk insurance in a region defined as a 'high risk area' had shot up, and later on, many companies began providing private armed guards for ships. Insurance companies sold millions of dollars' worth of additional insurance to shipping companies across the world for such troubled sea routes. Security companies started employing defence personnel who had retired early, while discarded war weapons sold in the secondary market were bought for the use of security guards. Of course, all of this was well implemented in a secure manner under the best management practices under maritime organizations' guidelines, always keeping in mind the safety of the ship and crew, but it opened a big opportunity to a handful of players. In the years since the hijacking of the *RAK Afrikana*, private armed guards protecting the ships crossing these waters has been a major reason why hijacking has come down drastically. And these private armed guards don't come cheap.

Even after learning all this, my thoughts today go back to the living conditions of the people doing the risky legwork. I can't help but wonder about the future of their children and their country. Whether by choice or under the weight of adverse circumstances, generation after generation is entering this life of violence. The lack of education, a stable national government and employment opportunities have created a vortex that the people of Somalia are being sucked into.

It is hard to differentiate cause from effect when things are part of a vicious cycle. On the one hand, it appears that there is no hope for the future—neither for their children and nor for their country. But on the other, it is this very violence that is blocking their chances of building a peaceful and prosperous future.

A short conversation with one of the young pirates left such a big impression on me that I doubt I'll ever forget it.

This kid, who had come on board in the later months of our captivity, would always walk around with Mohammed, the storekeeper. He was called Abdu, and his communication skills could be called okay, which was better than a lot of others. Abdu was not arrogant yet and felt he was still learning the tricks of his new trade.

What caught my eye was his gun—it was yet another AK-47, but unlike the rest, it was shiny and seemed new. One night, four people were sitting in the officers' mess room just before the lights were about to go out—Omar, Mohammed, Abdu and I. Omar had asked me to come and help him pick out a good action movie from the DVD collection. They were talking to each other in their language when Omar saw me staring at Abdu's gun.

'You want?' Omar asked me.

'Ha, I wish,' I replied.

'You want gun, you eat khat,' Omar said next.

I smiled and decided to voice my curiosity. 'Why is his gun so shiny, while your and Mohammed's are so dirty?'

Pat came the reply from Abdu. 'This gun, I get gift my birthday. My mother give gift on my eighteen birthday. She say go earn money.'

I was speechless. Now, I was staring at Abdu instead of the gun, and he was smiling while chewing his khat.

8

Our New Neighbours

It was a regular morning, nearly six months into our captivity. Every crew member on board was engaged in some activity or the other. I was sitting in a corner of the bridge, watching a game of chess between SK and Bade. Suddenly, we heard a gunshot.

By that stage of our ordeal, the sound of a bullet racing through the barrel of a gun, by itself, was not alarming—we had gotten used to it. But it wasn't comforting either.

As soon as I heard the sound, I looked up towards the monkey island. We could hear the pirate standing there jumping for joy; his screams of delight confirmed it a little while later.

As I stepped out of the bridge, I could still see the barrel of his gun smoking. There was nobody around him, so he must have fired the shot in the air. I also knew their protocol of firing a round whenever they saw any activity in the sea, so I figured he must have seen a boat or a ship. What baffled me was his joyous jumping. What in the ocean had made him so happy?

The number of pirates on board at this stage had reduced to between twelve and fifteen, for both day and night shifts combined. Within a few minutes of the shot, all the pirates on board had gathered on the deck.

From our camp, Chief Officer Ali Baig and a few other crew members assembled. Second Officer Parjeet had barely stepped on to the deck when the pirate on the bridge made a gesture by bringing two fingers close to his eyes and then pointing them away from his face towards the sea. We had seen the pirates make the same gesture in the past—it was a sign for binoculars. We couldn't imagine anybody using that sign to represent binoculars; it was peculiar and absurd.

Nevertheless, Parjeet handed the pirate his binoculars, while others who had them started looking too. The pirates had captured another ship, and it was approaching a few miles away. We could make out its size and shape—it was a tanker, a bitumen carrier from the looks of it.

Baig explained to us that it was their first 'catch' after the monsoon, and looked to be a big vessel, which is why the pirate on the monkey island had been jumping for joy.

Capt. Ram was standing on the port side, looking at the Captain's chair, which was on the starboard side bridge wing near the communication radio. Every ship has one Captain's chair; ours used to be in the centre of the bridge during our sailing days, but the pirates had moved it to the starboard side bridge wing the first day they had come on board. Now, after so many months, it didn't even look like a chair—the cover and cushion were torn, and the foam protruded from all sides. Capt. Ram had stopped sitting on it long back and nobody dared to asked him why. I felt it was because he knew he didn't have command on the *RAK Afrikana* any more, and also, he probably thought the pirates were abusing it by sitting on it without understanding the hard work it took for somebody to earn it. However, no cadet, crew member or officer ever sat on it, out of respect for the Captain.

Capt. Ram didn't look at the approaching ship through binoculars, but even with his naked eye, he spotted something and told Baig, '*Abey, chhota jahaaz hai* (Hey, it's a small ship).'

It took around thirty minutes for the ship to come parallel to ours, and then we could see clearly that Capt. Ram was right. The ship was in bad condition, requiring immediate attention and maintenance. At that moment, the pirates' excitement seemed misplaced and ignorant to us. Clearly, they were happy because they were anticipating good returns from the catch, but looking at the condition of the ship, we knew better as it was not very different from ours.

Naturally, the pirates wanted both of their cherished possessions close by, so they anchored the other ship not too far from ours. Our thoughts now turned to the crew on board that vessel; we couldn't help but think about what they must be going through. After all, we had been in the same position just a few months ago. Our thoughts about them became all the more sincere when we heard their voices on the radio.

Most ships use the same radio frequencies for on-board communication. When this ship was anchoring, we could hear their communication from the bridge to the anchor station. We learnt that most of the crew was from the Indian subcontinent, adding to our deep sense of empathy for them. We were two groups of people destined to experience the same struggles. In addition to the sentiment of kinship, their presence also gave us hope of getting released soon. The scale of the hijacking crisis had just got bigger because more people were now involved, so we imagined that somebody would take steps to resolve the crisis as soon as possible.

Nonetheless, while we were still in the middle of our own struggles, the state of affairs on the other ship started affecting us. Initially, we noticed that all the lights on that ship were fully operational after sundown. The crew and pirates on board had not yet started rationing their resources, as they should have. We had faced the same challenge after a few months in captivity, and sooner or later, they were going to realize it too. The arrival of the new ship made us think of all these challenges we had overcome. Over the course of our time in captivity, survival got tougher and tougher. The smallest things that we had never paid heed to earlier started becoming important. The earlier months of our hijacking, when there was no shortage of food or electricity, the situation, despite being tense, didn't affect our mental strength as much. Our stomachs were full and we were sleeping in air-conditioned rooms. But as time passed and weeks stretched to months, life slowly got tougher.

From showering once in three days to conserve water, to saving soap only for washing ourselves when we went to take a dump, to using toothpaste no more than just one drop a day, the long days started taking a toll on us. And then it came to a point where there was only enough fresh water for cooking and drinking. So we started taking a shower in sea water every day and in the end use just a bit of freshwater to rinse ourselves off.

For now, it looked like the other ship had all their supplies available, but that could change any time. Did they have a watermaker, or would they depend on the shore for the most basic human necessity—drinking water? I can't imagine what it would have been like if, apart from our other problems, we had to struggle for drinking water too. It wasn't as if the people controlling us with their guns had shown excellent management skills.

We didn't have to wait long to find out. After around a month, which was sooner than we had anticipated, our worst fears for the other ship came true, and the after-effects of the crisis spilled over to our ship too. The one thing we had going for us—potable water—got scarcer.

One day, the pirates came to us and demanded 200 litres more than they would take every day. They asked us to produce the same extra quantity every day, though they didn't tell us why. It was only later that we learnt they were sending it to the other ship because it had run out of drinking water.

When we learnt about their water crisis, we were glad to help. But the repercussions were deadly for both ships, because even though we had to produce extra water, we were not given extra diesel to run the generator for longer. This meant these 200 litres had to come out of our own supply. Our water filters were already working at full capacity, and we were desalinating by cleaning and drying out the same filters. In fact, Abdullah the Bosun was under strict orders not to let anyone else other than him touch the filters, and thanks to him, things had been running fine until now. But now, it was only a matter of time before the filters stopped working, and when they did, we weren't going to get fresh ones.

Capt. Ram called a meeting to discuss the sharing of freshwater with the other vessel. Every crew member was present, and he started by sharing his thoughts about somehow reaching out to our neighbours and telling them about rationing their resources. But this was impossible. So, the plan became to cut our own consumption to help them. Capt. Ram was the first one who volunteered to reduce his quota, and instructed Parjeet and Third Officer Kuldeep to do the same. I really marvelled at, even envied, this quality in him.

Bada Sahab, the Chief Engineer, tried to retain his quota by saying that he needed to bathe every day before prayers, but his immediate junior, Mir Balach, countered the point by saying that the Almighty accepted exemptions when one was in troubled circumstances. Abdullah, meanwhile, ensured the entire crew agreed, and even the cooking was managed without much difficulty. It was great to see that even after seven tough months in captivity, we remained considerate enough to share this precious resource with the other seafarers who shared in our fate.

At this moment, you might be thinking why there was so much fuss over just 200 litres of water. But life had shown us that every drop of water and every gram of food could save a life.

Within a few weeks, more and more ships came in, till the area looked like an anchorage. The next vessel that joined us was a small fishing boat whose crew seemed to be from

Southeast Asia, but it sailed out again immediately with pirates on board to catch a bigger ship.

Then came a huge container ship belonging to one of the biggest lines in the world, the Mediterranean Shipping Company (MSC). This vessel came in towing a barge, which is a flat cargo carrier that can be manned or unmanned. This one was unmanned.

The story, we learnt, was that the barge, which was loaded with pipes and some other cargo that was difficult to make out, was being towed by a smaller tugboat. When the pirates attacked, they reached the barge first and boarded it. This was an easy task because such towage is not a high-speed operation, and the height of the barge is not far above the pirates' boat. The pirates hadn't seen that the crew was all in the tugboat, which could have been up to 200 metres ahead, depending on the speed and the weather out at sea. Thus, the crew had enough time to disengage the tow rope and leave the barge behind. The tug could do decent speed without towing the barge, so it managed to escape and leave the pirates on the unmanned barge. But the pirates weren't going to leave anything behind if it could float, so when the captured container ship sailed near them, they got it to tow the barge and brought it to our location. So now, there were three ships—ours, the bitumen carrier and the container ship—anchored there, while the fishing boat returned and was tied to our ship as it did not have an anchor.

Every night, the new catches would be lit up fully, while we would be spending the night in darkness.

The fishing boat then left again, and this time, we had to give them some of our freshwater as well. We felt like we had become the local water suppliers—the pirates would just come and tell us how much water they needed that day, and we would do the best we could for our safety and that of the other ships' crews. This time the fishing boat didn't return, and we didn't bother to check why, but many months later, I found out it had nearly reached the west coast of India—almost 1,500 to 1,800 nautical miles away—where it was apprehended by the Indian Coast Guard. About forty pirates were captured on board.

Around nine months after our hijacking, another chemical tanker joined us. Now, the area of the sea where each ship can be anchored differs according to the vessel's size, and all the ships I've mentioned so far were roughly similar sizes to ours, so they were anchored around us. From time to time, we could hear the pirates talking to each other on the ships' radios, and then, they started their horn-blowing game again.

One afternoon, when the pirates were playing their horn game, SK, Bade and I stepped out on to the bridge wing to share a cigarette. We had made an arrangement among ourselves that we would smoke our first and last cigarettes of the day individually, but share the rest, because supply was limited. Out of respect for Capt. Ram, we also avoided smoking if there was a chance that he would see us. But as we smoked and pulled each other's leg that day, Capt. Ram walked into view, and we went from 'at ease' to 'attention' within a second.

Thankfully, the Captain was in a fun mood that day, and wondered aloud why SK and I addressed Anubhav as 'Bade'. Only SK and I called him that, because we had been together since our pre-sea days, and Anubhav was the oldest of us in age. He had joined our pre-sea batch a little while after SK and me, and by that time, we had gotten familiar with our schedules. One day, when Anubhav was late during an early-morning muster meeting, our instructor had asked about him and SK had replied, 'Sir, *bade bhaiya thoda* slow *hain* (Sir, big brother is a little slow).' Over time, 'Bade Bhaiya' got shortened to 'Bade'.

Capt. Ram joined in our laughter, but then changed the topic. 'With so many ships around us now, my hopes have gone up that maybe our negotiations will be fast-tracked. Maybe now the time is coming for us to leave this place. My hopes are high. All you boys have spent this time very bravely. Hang on for a few more days,' he advised. We listened to him, and with our hands behind our backs, nodded a 'yes, sir'.

None of us knew that the worst was yet to come. Yes, we did get out of that place a few months after this conversation, but not before experiencing hell on earth.

The first bit of bad news came in when Jafar received a call from land—most probably from Tarjuman. The caller had been informed by our ship's owner of the untimely death of the wife of our welder Lucas (whom we called Luca Baba).

I had not seen a more calm and polite personality than Luca Baba. A tall, slim, muscular man with a bald head, big eyes and a bigger smile permanently on his face, he was someone who always said 'yes' to work.

When Capt. Ram was informed about the death, he called Abdullah and Luca to the bridge to break the news. Luca didn't show any reaction when he heard of his wife's passing; he just fell silent and returned to the crew mess room. For two days, nobody saw his face. He had no means to check if this news was accurate, or how and when it had happened. He could do nothing about it; he had no control over his circumstances. But when he appeared a couple of days later, he stood strong. I got a chance to express my condolences, but he told me, '*Baana*, don't worry. I am sure we will go back. God can't be so ruthless to so many of us. You have your family; I have my kids. We have to live for them. God is watching. He will get us back to them.'

9

Lurking Danger

Being sailors, it was normal for us to be out at sea for a long time, but these weren't 'normal' conditions we were being held under.

I believe one of the attributes of human nature that made us survive our ordeal was our ability to adapt and coexist. In situations such as ours, it is said that the spirit of survival always overpowers thoughts of death. And so it was with us—even under those irregular and desperate circumstances, we had found our will to survive.

Over time, a semblance of normalcy began to appear on the ship. Though there were still captors and captives on board, the lines dividing us were getting blurred in some ways, thanks to open communication from both sides.

One afternoon, seven months since we had been confined to the ship, I was standing on the bridge deck looking at the open sea in front of me. By now, Jafar and I were having quite a few conversations around this time of day, because I had made it part of my routine to step out to the bridge deck and take in some sun before starting my workout. Jafar came to talk to me that afternoon too, and this conversation turned out to be less informative and one-sided than the last one.

I had gotten used to Jafar's peculiar way of talking. In fact, most of the pirates communicated in a similar manner, which was very different from what we were used to—they would use hand gestures to make their point, along with the handful of English nouns and verbs they knew.

That day, too, when Jafar began to speak, he used only four words—tomorrow, come, good and news—and pointed to the shore. He was sure I would understand, and I did. The next day, his superiors would come to the ship from the shore, bearing good news. He emphasized the good news part.

By this point, the pirates' idea of good news had become a little stale for us. Ever since we had dropped anchor near the Somali coast, they had been talking about us getting good news from the shore almost every day, but nothing good ever happened, so after a while, we stopped getting our hopes up. On this day, Jafar expected that his words would make me happy, but they didn't. Nevertheless, I thought of informing Capt. Ram, so I went to the bridge.

The scene there had become very familiar, as all of us had subconsciously found our comfort spots. Capt. Ram always sat near the chart table, flanked by Second Officer Parjeet and Third Officer Kuldeep. Chief Officer Ali Baig would station himself near the entrance, while we cadets would sit or lie down on the floor. When I told Capt. Ram what Jafar had said, he, too, did not show any enthusiasm. 'Let them come, whoever it is. We welcome everyone on this ship anyway,' he said.

The rules for moving around the ship had been relaxed quite a bit by this point. The number of pirates had also reduced onboard. We had to just be careful to not do anything suspicious and keep the pirates informed about our whereabouts. Everyone enjoyed this bit of freedom and chose their spots. Batti Sahab, the electrician, spent most of his time with us cadets, while Second Engineer Mir Balach divided his time between his cabin and with us on the bridge or the deck. Third Engineer Ahmed Durrani, the aloof fellow, pretty much kept to himself, while Bada Sahab, the Chief Engineer, mostly relaxed in his cabin. Crew members were always near the galley or their accommodation. We cadets shuffled between the bridge during the day and the officers' mess at night.

However, despite all our scepticism, the next day, Jafar's words turned out to be true as a couple of boats did come from the shore. At the time, we were scattered all across the deck. When the people on the boats came on board, we saw most of them weren't familiar faces. However, I remembered one guy from the day of the hijacking—Aaden, the tallest of the pirates whom we had nicknamed Camel Face. He was carrying a big machine gun with a long belt of bullets.

We had barely made sense of the commotion when we heard that everybody had been asked to gather on the deck below the bridge. This was an order, so all of us stopped whatever we were doing and followed it. I quickly reached the spot, and saw everyone else pouring in from every corner of the ship. Chief Cook Muhammed also entered, whining like he always did. 'You don't understand, these are dangerous people,' he complained. We had also noticed him talking to himself quite a few times, so, to ensure that he didn't end up aggravating the pirates, Abdullah went up to him and told him to stop whining.

Then I spotted the pirate commander Abdi on board. He had returned to the ship after a couple of months.

All the pirates were carrying rifles and other guns, and rounded us up below the 'Safety First' stencil sign on deck, between the cargo hatch and the accommodation. We had no clue what was going on and why we were being summoned like that. We thought that perhaps they were delivering a message to everyone. But then, there were quicker and more efficient ways to do that through the bridge.

They asked all twenty-four of us to stand in two or three rows, one behind another. I was standing in the middle, and it reminded me of the end-of-year class photographs in school.

Abdi was going to address the crowd, and he had just begun talking when I heard a cry of pain from somewhere behind me. One of our oilers, Abdul Mbarawa, was crying out in pain. His body and shoulders had stiffened, his fingers had straightened out, his palms were positioned awkwardly and he was making irregular, pained sounds. It was obvious that the poor man was suffering from some sort of anxiety or epilepsy attack. This was baffling, because he had no history of any such ailment.

Capt. Ram and Abdullah rushed to him immediately, but before they could reach him, he fell to the floor. He was still conscious, eyes wide open as if in shock, but he wasn't responding. Naturally, the gathering, Abdi's speech and everything else took a back seat; all our attention was focused on the Abdul's plight now. He was in bad shape, and it was troubling for all of us to look at our crewmate going through that. We were all worried and scared.

The pirates surrounding us with guns were stunned too. Abdi looked surprised and clueless. But Camel Face reacted unexpectedly. Apparently, he assumed that Abdul was faking some sort of medical emergency, either for attention or to try and get out of the situation. While the other pirates were still trying to discern how to address the situation, Camel Face moved swiftly and pointed his weapon at the oiler, and repeatedly screamed, 'Up, up, up!'

He continued to charge at the stricken man, pointing and yelling. To his mind, this was all a charade. He didn't realize he was possibly scaring the oiler more with the weapon in his hand.

The situation had worsened enough already. I believe most of us wanted to help Abdul, but we were still overwhelmed, not to mention surrounded by people holding guns. Something had to be done. Finally, Abdullah intervened and approached Camel Face, who turned his gun on him. With folded hands, in a calm tone, Abdullah requested him to let the poor man be, and that there was no way he was faking such pain and misery. The oiler was indeed in serious trouble and might have died. I'd like to believe Abdullah's words fell on empathetic ears, because Abdi told Camel Face to back down, and he moved away.

We brought the unconscious oiler to a bench and laid him down on it. Bade managed to get some freshwater, and we sprinkled some on his face and tried to pour some into his mouth too. Despite our efforts, he remained in that condition for around thirty to forty-five minutes. We desperately waited for him to recover, and finally, when Capt. Ram realized the situation was under control, he instructed the chief cook and the steward to stay with him and assist him in any way that was needed.

As soon as things regained some semblance of normalcy, Abdi and his men swung into action. They rounded us up again, and the pirate commander started speaking. He told us they were going to click some photographs and send them to the ship's owner and media outlets to put pressure on them to release the ransom. I hadn't been far off the mark when I thought this reminded me of a class photo.

One of the other pirates brought a camera and composed the shot. He clicked a few pictures of us from different angles, with his armed cohorts covering their faces.

Suddenly, Abdi told him to stop, and looked at the camera from different angles. Then, he looked at the sky, and said something super confusing—addressing Capt. Ram, he claimed the camera's battery was dead, and the light here was not so good, so they'd have to take some of us to another ship to get the photographs clicked.

This didn't make much sense. If the battery was dead, why didn't they just get more batteries or another camera from the other ships? Also, it was afternoon, and the sun was quite bright, so why were they going through the trouble of transporting us to another vessel?

Nonetheless, we knew we were not in a position to question their plans or ideas, and kept our apprehensions to ourselves. Capt. Ram conveyed the message to us and asked us to prepare to deboard and go to another ship. Quite frankly, when I heard those words, a part of me wished to be one of the men deboarding. I imagined that this would be a change of scenery and I'd get a chance to see a new environment, possibly interact with some new people and get to know what it was like on the other hijacked ships.

Abdi, however, made the call to choose five individuals—Capt. Ram, Parjeet, Abdullah, Luca Baba and Senior Cadet Zaheer. And even though we had no say in the matter, Capt. Ram took a stand that none of them would leave the vessel without life jackets. He was really stern about it; it was a safety matter and he was not willing to take any risks.

So the five men prepared to deboard. Capt. Ram asked one of the cadets to get the life jackets from the bridge, and pointed at Bade. He went up to get the life jackets, but he was taking some time, so Parjeet called out to him. Crucially, though, he addressed him by his last name. 'Aarya, come fast!' he said.

When Abdi heard the last name, it caught his attention. Parjeet didn't realize what he had done unintentionally, until he heard Abdi repeat the name 'Aarya'. It was then that Parjeet uttered an 'Oh, fuck' in horror.

Clearly, the pirates were aware that the ship's owner was Capt. Aarya. It was merely a coincidence that Bade and the owner shared a last name, but Abdi assumed he was his son or relative, and that was leverage he didn't intend to let go of. We tried to explain that Aarya was a common last name in India, just like there were in other countries, including Somalia. We tried to point out just how many unrelated Mohammeds there were on the ship at this moment. But Abdi wasn't listening, he was focused on strengthening his negotiating position, so he insisted that Bade join the party deboarding the ship.

All six of them, accompanied by Abdi and a couple of more pirates, went down the ladder to the boat, which we stared at till it sailed out of sight. We thought they would be back in an hour or so, but when they didn't come back for a couple of hours, we started to get concerned.

Moreover, we were nearing sunset. The boat was supposed to come back and leave for the shore before that, because they had never once left the ship after the sun had gone down. If there wasn't enough light, would the boat come back that day? What if it didn't come back at all? What if this was a trick played by the pirates, who had taken our shipmates with the intention of never bringing them back? We didn't have any way for these questions to be answered, so we just waited.

They had left around 2.30 p.m., and now three hours had passed. This was when our concerns turned to full-blown worry. We had no clue what was happening on that other ship. How were our people doing? I believe everybody was wondering these same things when we heard Chief Officer Baig announce that a boat was approaching our ship. We ran towards the bridge window to have a look, but the boat was still far away. 'Is everyone on that boat? And why is it coming from the direction of the shore?' asked Mir Balach from behind us.

We needed binoculars to make sure, but earlier today, the pirates had confiscated all of ours, so it was not possible to identify the occupants. All we could see were the reflectors on the life jackets, so we deduced that these were indeed our people coming back. But were all six of them on board? There was no way to know yet.

The boat crossed over to the other side of our ship, and some time later, we saw our shipmates coming up the ladder. Capt. Ram was the first, and he went directly to the bridge, lit a cigarette, sat down on the floor facing away from the sea and gave strict instructions to not be disturbed for a while. I didn't see Abdullah and Luca Baba; perhaps they had gone directly to the crew accommodation. Parjeet and Zaheer came next, and then finally we saw Bade.

Obviously, we were all curious about the delay and about what had happened in the interim. Plus, why were they returning from a different direction? Nobody dared to violate Capt. Ram's direct instructions; Parjeet was quiet; and I didn't want to talk to Zaheer because he was known to exaggerate everything. I couldn't help but notice that the others had all lit cigarettes as soon as they had returned to the bridge.

So I turned to Bade for details. I went and sat beside him and joked, 'Bade, they didn't do anything unspeakable to you, did they?'

Bade turned his face towards me and glared. This was clearly not the time to joke. He shook his head. He seemed speechless. I realized that he was probably in shock. I asked him if he wanted to step out and smoke too, but he just got up and walked to the bridge deck.

Everyone else on the ship was stunned at the condition of the men who had returned, and so, for more than an hour, there was absolute silence on the ship. No one moved from their spots.

The lights were turned on after a while, and we had to go back to our duty of filling and storing freshwater. The crew had started making preparations for dinner. Everything seemed to be business as usual, but in our hearts, we knew it wasn't. The profound difference was the absence of any noise, because usually, while performing these chores, a lot of us talked to each other.

As we fetched the water, I saw Abdullah sitting in the middle of our path. There was a lot of movement around him, but his eyes and mind didn't seem to register any of it.

It was only after dinner was served and we had all sat down to eat in the officers' mess that Bade finally opened up, while Parjeet narrated the tale on the bridge. We pieced together the entire story from these two separate narratives.

Once our crewmates left the ship, the boat had gone towards another ship for a while, but then changed course and started moving towards the shore. The six of them got really startled when they learnt they were not going to the ship. What about the photographs? Would they be clicked on land now?

When the boat reached the shore, all of them were asked to get out and head to a spot where some SUVs were parked. The pirates who had accompanied them on the boat were joined by a few more, as well as Tarjuman, who was the only one of them not carrying a gun.

He greeted Capt. Ram, saying, 'I am sorry but we need to send a message to the owners, as we find them not cooperating with our demands. Seems they don't care about you at all.'

Tarjuman looked at Abdi and said something in their language. Abdi replied and then pointed at Bade and mentioned 'Aarya'.

The six captives were then told to kneel at an arm's distance from each other, and their hands were tied behind their backs. So far, all the instructions being given by Tarjuman and Abdi to their cohorts were in their language, but then, Abdi said in English, 'Soldiers! Take position!'

It must have been terrifying. The crew members had left the ship for a picture, and here they were, on their knees, seeing a few men load their guns and point them at their heads. Was this really happening? They had not anticipated it. What had gone wrong for the pirates to resort to such violence? They were about to murder six people in cold blood!

Abdi gave another little hand gesture, and a pirate covered each of their heads with the sort of black cloth hoods that are used for hangings. Everything was happening too fast, and before any of our crew could get a grip, their vision was blocked. Now, they could only hear and sense things around them, but not see.

Tarjuman's last words were, 'I am sorry, gentlemen, I tried.' Next, they heard Abdi shout, 'Soldiers! Fire!'

Shots were heard all around, and none of the captives had any idea who was being shot and who would be next. Each of them believed that the ones to their sides had been shot dead, and that it was their turn next.

Suddenly, the firing stopped and Bade was grabbed by the neck and dragged to a car, still with the cloth hood covering his head and his hands tied behind his back. Finally, when he was shoved inside and the hood was removed, Bade saw

Capt. Ram and Abdi sitting next to him. Tarjuman was sitting in the front passenger seat, while the back seat of the SUV was occupied by another pirate with a gun. The Captain and Bade were both rattled, shocked and confused.

'We killed the others. They are disposing of the dead bodies now,' Tarjuman told them. 'You call your owner and he pays the money now.'

Tarjuman connected the call, and Capt. Ram spoke to the owner in a pleading manner, with tears in his eyes. 'Six of us were brought to the shore at gunpoint, and I have no idea where the others are. I am helpless,' the Captain said. Bade admitted to us that he had never seen the Captain plead like he had in that moment. Even after learning that four of his crew members had just been shot dead, Capt. Ram mustered up the courage to speak about the incident and convey the pirates' demands to the ship owner.

After the call, the Captain and Bade were driven back to the same spot where the shooting had taken place. They were still trembling and trying to get a hold of themselves. Now they were to be sent back to the *RAK Afrikana*.

Bade said he had all sorts of thoughts rushing through his head, but when they arrived at the boat that would take them back to the ship, they were stunned—the other four crew members were there, alive. Trembling and scared, but alive. They were going back 'home', because the ship where they were being held hostage felt like home to them in that moment.

Among the rest of the crew, there was a sense of relief, knowing that it had all been a ploy and no real harm had come to anybody. But the incident changed a lot on the ship, affecting as it did the men who had experienced this first-hand, and the others, like me, who had remained on the ship but had heard our colleagues' ordeal. Something broke in our minds, and silence engulfed our ship for the next couple of weeks. Chores, responsibilities and jobs went on, but the smiles disappeared from our faces. There was an abominable lull.

The incident brought some of us out of our complacency. Now we knew that the threat to our lives was real, and that guns could be fired at any moment and that any of us could be lost forever. Whatever equation some of us had developed with the pirates over the last seven months changed drastically. The lines between 'us' and 'them', which had started blurring over time, were drawn back again, in indelible ink. The behaviour of the pirates towards us changed too.

We had been hijacked long ago, but until that incident, we hadn't experienced anything this dangerous. Sure, it had been challenging, but there had been no real act of violence. This changed everything.

We weren't aware of whether the pirates' ruse had worked. As far as we knew, the negotiations were still not moving in the direction they wanted. There was no clarity on when we were going to be released, if ever.

The sun still shone brightly in the sky, but for us even darker days lay ahead.

10

Prepare to Go Hunting

What had happened to our friends on land lingered in our minds. During those days, I used to spend the afternoons sitting in a makeshift shade we had built in the aft near the mooring winch and connected to the railing using the fishing line. It was a nice sitting lounge kind of area, utilized when fishing. There were a few damaged benches and other repurposed 'furniture' to relax in the shade.

As I have mentioned before, my slippers were torn in places, so one afternoon, I was sitting in the shade stitching them. I was thinking about the aspirations my parents had had for me after my misadventures in Canada, hoping I would find a stable path in life. And here I was, stitching slippers while being held captive on a ship.

Mohammed, the pirates' storekeeper, was checking their food supplies when he saw me and came down to sit next to me. Diverting my attention from the slippers, he asked in a friendly manner, and I paraphrase, 'The owner of this ship must have made plenty of money through it, since the ship has been running for so long. Why doesn't he want to pay money, then?'

By now, I had made sense of the business model of hijacking merchant ships, and I knew that in our case, the way negotiations were going, the pirates were not pleased. Our extended stay had increased their budgeted expenditure, and the return on investment was nowhere in sight. They were clearly getting restless, because our ordeal had lasted longer than they expected, and the gamble they took in keeping us there and not leaving the Somali coast empty during the monsoons had not paid off. They hadn't hijacked anything during the monsoon, and what they had taken after the rains hadn't started paying off yet.

I wanted to be careful in replying to Mohammed's question, because who knew how he might misinterpret my words, and what news would reach the other pirates. Also, when he asked me the question, I knew he had nothing to do until evening and had come to kill time. I do come from a family of professors and teachers but I don't think I have received enough of those genes to have had much patience for Mohammed.

Therefore, I took a pause and then sidestepped the question by saying 'no idea', and went back to the slippers.

I hadn't expected what he did next. The pirates all knew how deprived we were of supplies, so this clever guy took out a pack of cigarettes. I knew he didn't smoke, but when he offered one to me, I asked him, 'When did you start?' He replied, 'Not me, Omar.' Then he mimed giving it back when Omar woke up.

I took a cigarette without further questions, and as soon as I lit it, Mohammed repeated his question. He had me in his trap now.

I tried to explain by giving an example. 'You buy a taxi and drive it for two years, then sell it to Omar. He drives it for two years and then sells to Abdi. He drives it for one year and then I catch Abdi and tell him, "Your taxi worked five years, you have so much money." But the taxi was with Abdi only for one year. Abdi has no money. Same with our owner and this ship.'

Till date, I cannot guarantee if he understood even one word, but I made it look so complicated that he just got up, nodded and walked back inside.

This might have just been a casual conversation between people from the two camps, but then it emerged that the pirates had already started speculating internally about their options.

Within a week, when we woke up one morning, we noticed a lot of movement on the ship. We had got used to quiet mornings with occasional turbulence, so to speak, but this was different. I saw Tarjuman on board, moving around with a lot of new people. There was also movement on the side of the ship—a few boats had come loaded with large quantities of diesel, and we were asked to assist in bringing the containers on board. We noticed the quantity was more than what we usually received for the generator, and the timing was also unusual, because on other days, the supply came just before sunset.

Even after all that we had gone through, my first thought was still a positive one. With so much movement of people and supplies, I thought we might just be released. Maybe they were going to receive the ransom and were preparing to give us the minimum supplies we would need to reach the closest port.

It wasn't just me; the thought of going back home had brought renewed vigour to the other cadets too. Even when we were pulling up all that fuel from the boat to our ship, we could feel an increase in strength and a boost in morale. I felt a potent adrenaline rush. But in all this action, we had forgotten who we were dealing with.

Once the fuel and the supplies were on board, Abdullah came up to the aft deck with us, and I asked him, 'You think we are going?' He kept a straight face, didn't make eye contact, made a clicking sound from his mouth to indicate a negative and continued blowing out smoke, before Second Officer Parjeet called him to the bridge.

Tarjuman and Capt. Ram were up on the monkey island while one of the pirates stood guard on the staircase leading up to it. Soon, we were informed that Capt. Ram had summoned everyone to go to the monkey island one by one. We didn't know what was going on. Our excitement about getting released was now mixed with the fear of uncertainty. Why were we being summoned to the monkey island like that? What was going on? Were we even getting released? If not, why this sudden influx of hundreds of gallons of fuel?

Soon, we got to know that each member of the crew was being asked to call their families. This, for some reason, got my hopes back up. I thought they might be wanting us to tell our families we were fine and would be coming home soon. I had no idea how that would work, but I just felt like sticking to positive thoughts. But as the last of the non-cadets, Rashid the steward, came down disappointed, and it was our turn to go up, we had a clear sense that it wasn't the good news we had all been hoping for.

Senior Cadet David was the first in line to go up, and upon his return, narrated what was happening, which the other crew hadn't done. Apparently, there had been no progress in the ransom talks and now Tarjuman was asking us to call our families, the idea being to put some pressure on our national governments through our parents, hoping the authorities would intervene and pay the ransom instead of the owner. Everybody was instructed to speak in English only, not in their native tongues.

Now that we knew what lay ahead, the thought of speaking to our families after such a long time flooded our minds with all kinds of mixed emotions. I was still awaiting my turn in the queue when Zaheer came down and told us he had spoken to his father. In his voice, I could sense the emotional struggle, and at the same time the relief that he had felt. I am sure his family would have felt the same way.

Senior Cadet Krishna was next, and despite Tarjuman's strict instructions about sticking to English, when he reached the monkey island and was handed the phone to call his family, he started speaking to them in fast-paced Malayalam. Tarjuman immediately objected; hearing incomprehensible words made him nervous. But Krishna told us later it hadn't been easy for the big man to get up from his sitting position and snatch the phone back, so by the time he did, Krishna had told his mother what he had to say. Tarjuman questioned him about it, and Krishna replied, 'My family doesn't speak English.'

Think about it, if an individual living at gunpoint for eight months finally gets to speak to his family, would he spill secrets or would he just try and live in that moment of hearing their voices? Not just Krishna, Zaheer or Samit, I am sure the only message everyone must have passed on to their families was that they were healthy and doing well. What else could we tell them, anyway? There was no point sharing our struggles with our families. They were going through enough as it was.

Finally it was my turn. When I got upstairs, I saw Capt. Ram sitting on a chair while Tarjuman was sitting on the floor with a backrest, wearing his usual tights and vest, chewing khat as he asked me to make the call. In that moment, I was stuck in a dilemma. It was not that I didn't want to speak to my parents—God knows I did—but there were a couple of challenges. First, I simply had no idea of the current whereabouts of my family. In our last conversation, when I was in Seychelles and my family in Dubai, my father had mentioned he was about to get transferred to the main campus of his university as vice chancellor. If that had happened, my mother and he had most likely gone to India. Second, if he was still in Dubai, I didn't want to call him there because that would have revealed my connection to the city where the owner of the ship was based. I had no clue what the repercussions could be if the pirates knew my family lived in Dubai, especially after the incident with Bade having the same last name as the owner. So I made the tough decision not to call my parents.

Tarjuman sensed my apprehension and asked if I had no home phone number. I replied that I didn't remember the numbers; that everything had been saved on my phone and his people had taken that away on day one. Truthfully, the only phone number I remembered was that of my maternal grandparents in Dehradun, and initially, the thought of calling them did occur to me, but I decided otherwise. Later, I learnt that it was a wise decision because they had been kept completely unaware of my ordeal due to their age.

This act by the pirates made it clear that we were not getting released. We learnt later that all the fuel had been sent to our ship because they were preparing to set sail and hunt other ships. Since monsoon was on its way out, using the *RAK Afrikana* as a mother vessel, they hoped to cover more distance and catch a minimum of two other ships. If they were successful, they would accept the owner's current offer and release us.

Discussions about this plan took place between Capt. Ram and Tarjuman on the monkey island. The Captain tried his best to explain that our engine was in bad shape. He pointed out to Tarjuman that for the last eight months, we had been anchored here without any movement or maintenance, so it would be risky. The Captain's mantra was always safety of the crew and the ship first. But the pirates didn't listen to him.

To make things worse, our Chief Engineer, Bada Sahab, readily agreed with the pirates and even called it a good idea.

In reality, it was going to be anything but easy, because, as you'll remember, this whole episode had begun because our engine had stopped due to a technical issue. The cause was actually never discovered, let alone fixed. It was ironic that what had made our ship vulnerable to piracy in the first place was now going to be a hurdle in our release as well.

Capt. Ram again tried his best to explain all this to Tarjuman and the other pirates, but it fell on deaf ears.

Bada Sahab, as I have mentioned before, had spent all these months trying to be in the pirates' good books. When Tarjuman and the others had a discussion with him about the fuel status, keeping Capt. Ram out of the loop, Bada Sahab told them he was sure there was no diesel hidden anywhere and that he would need a good amount of diesel to try and run the engine. The rest of the crew was aghast when we got to know about Bada Sahab agreeing with such ideas. Bada Sahab had gotten in the habit of agreeing with the pirates about everything. This gave the pirates more confidence about their impractical ideas, and we sensed this would backfire on us someday.

We had a good amount of HFO (Heavy Fuel Oil) in reserve, but the main engines of ships can't run on them from the start. They have to start on diesel and then shift to HFO when out at sea, where manoeuvring is lesser. The same diesel is needed for power generators on the ship. However, the pirates were under the impression that HFO would be enough to run the ship's main engine. It took Capt. Ram a while to explain to Tarjuman why HFO alone would not be enough and how we would need diesel as well, which

Tarjuman translated to Abdi and his boss on the shore. The surprising part was that whatever Capt. Ram had explained was cross-verified with Bada Sahab by the pirates and it was only after his nod that they believed Capt. Ram.

The pirates decided to bring diesel from the shore, but were not happy as this would mean more money and resources to be spent. But at this stage they were trusting Bada Sahab more than anyone else on the ship to get the engines working. So all those gallons that we were lifting with enthusiasm were not for our release but to go on a hunt.

Bada Sahab and his team took a couple of days to prepare the engine room, and then he finally confirmed to Abdi that he was ready to test the engine. I was on the telegraph on the bridge, while the Second Officer was on radar watch. Chief Officer Ali Baig was at the fo'c'sle with the Bosun and a few deck crew were heaving up the anchor and communicating with the bridge on the radio.

Capt. Ram issued the order, 'Dead slow ahead!' I pushed the lever and said, 'Dead slow ahead, sir!' Repeating the command is the process to confirm that the instructed action has been taken.

The engine started, and as we felt the vibrations, it was a surreal experience. After so many months on a stationary ship, the thrumming engine gave us a sense of movement and direction, raising our hopes that things would get better. But it was just a tingling of our senses and nothing more. Baig on the radio confirmed, 'Anchor Aweigh, Captain', but the ship, instead of moving forward, started drifting backwards because of the current. The container ship anchored behind us blew its horn to warn us. Capt. Ram told Baig on the radio, 'Chief, let go of starboard anchor.'

This process was repeated for a couple of days—Bada Sahab would try the engine for a few hours, burn some diesel, but achieve no movement. I started calling the whole process a 'telegraph drill', since I would just stand there and keep moving the lever of the telegraph as per Capt. Ram's orders while the rest of us on the bridge continued to be disappointed. Abdi was getting frustrated by this, and when he couldn't get things moving, one of the guys higher up the food chain came on board. His name was Ahmed, and from the day he arrived, the pirates' friendly conversations towards us and between themselves vanished. They were on their best behaviour, and even stopped fighting over khat and cigarettes.

Ahmed was a tall, broad-shouldered man who had a bit of a belly and kept his beard in the same style as Jafar. He spoke good English and seemed to be a fast learner.

Wearing red shorts and a white vest, with a black shawl wrapped around his upper body, a cigarette in hand and an AK-47 hanging on his shoulder, as soon as he stepped on board, he wanted to visit the engine room before coming to the bridge. But he did not want to go with any of the engineers—he wanted one of the oilers. Hassan Idris accompanied him. He was the first pirate who dared to enter the engine room without showing any fear. He walked around every corner of the room, manually checked the valves to see if they were open or shut, and kept asking Hassan which valves were for which pipeline. Hassan must have been in the engine room with Ahmed for close to three hours and when they walked out, Ahmed asked Hassan, 'So you are really sinking?'

When destiny is not on your side, the chances of anything good happening are washed out and the bad starts becoming worse. In one of our cargo hatches, we had a hole and water had started seeping in. We were not very sure from which section of the hatch, because it was full of cargo (cement in jumbo bags), but we assumed it was the hole in the ship's hull that had been plugged in Karachi. Our ship was listing (tilting) towards the starboard side and this hole was also in the starboard section below cargo hatch number two, where we observed that the water level had started rising. At this stage it was still not as alarming, and every night when the generator would start, we would use the bilge pumps inside the cargo hatch to pump the water out and bring the ship back to even keel, which is when a ship is not listing or tilting to one side.

Ahmed was now on the bridge. Capt. Ram and I were repeating the telegraph drill on the bridge, while Bada Sahab was down in the engine room trying to see if any movement was possible in front of Ahmed, who sat in the starboard corner with his khat and some drinks, monitoring everything.

Out of nowhere, Ahmed asked the Captain, 'How many children do you have?'

Capt. Ram replied, 'One daughter.'

'Only one? Why? I have sixteen children from three wives!' said Ahmed.

'I do not make enough money to feed those many people,' replied the Captain.

'I don't feed them; it is God who feeds them,' replied Ahmed.

'Then, God will also move this ship,' retorted the Captain.

Ahmed's face showed that he didn't like the sarcasm, but he just dropped the conversation and sat back to monitor.

Multiple attempts were made to crank the engine, but when there was still no movement, Bada Sahab, to save face, started speculating about the possible reasons for this. We could see from the deck that there was a disturbance in the water every time the engine started and rotated the propellor blades, and there were, of course, the vibrations. So, Bada Sahab thought there must be marine growth, which is why when changing the pitch (of the propeller blades, which help in forward and backward movement of the ship), it was not able to produce enough thrust for movement.

This explanation was highly improbable, because if there was marine growth on the propeller, it would wash out easily once the blades started moving. But assuming there was such growth, how could it be cleared?

The bigger the ship, the bigger the propeller, and for a ship the size of ours, it would've been as big as a human being, maybe even bigger. The propeller is positioned a few metres beneath the water level, and as its blades rotate, they cut through the water and produce thrust for moving forward or backward.

The propellers are cleaned either with the help of specialized diving equipment or when the ship is at dry dock. But the pirates started planning how to get this task accomplished, since Bada Sahab had pointed this out and he was their only friend on board. Plus, his knowledge seemed to amaze them.

Bada Sahab agreed that things would be better if the propeller was cleaned, and recommended that somebody from the ship go down in a boat to try and reach it. When Ahmed told the Captain the idea and confirmed it came from Bada Sahab, the Captain lost it and gave the senior officer a piece of his mind. He made sure he spoke in Hindi, but Ahmed understood by the tone that the Captain was not willing to go along with this idea. No competent seafarer would, because it was risky. Bada Sahab replied to the Captain in Urdu that he thought Ahmed would send one of the pirates to do the job, and Capt. Ram just said, '*Bewakoof ho kya aap* (Are you an idiot)?'

However, the pirates' guns forced the Captain's hand, so he put his foot down that he would go down into the boat too. 'I will not let anyone go alone!' he insisted.

Finally, a boat was prepared for the task, and a long stick was fashioned to scrape the vegetation off the propeller. One member each from the pirates' and our camp got on the boat, accompanied by Capt. Ram wearing a life jacket. There was also another standby boat that went along to ensure the first couldn't sail away. The boats tried to reach the propeller with the long stick, but the current was just too strong; the laws of physics weren't letting the stick stay still long enough to reach the propeller. After spending hours in the sun trying the exercise multiple times with different approaches, they gave up and returned to the ship.

The problem was still not solved, though, and the pirates were eager to come up with another idea. This time, Ahmed improvised on the original suggestion and decided that somebody would have to dive into the water to do the job. The moment Capt. Ram heard this, he turned to glare at Bada Sahab. The Captain again tried to explain that it was not safe, and nobody should even attempt to do it, including the pirates. But he didn't actually have a say in the matter, because Ahmed was calling the shots, and to him, it looked like a simple task for a swimmer. So, he decided that somebody must dive.

Diving into the open sea is not as easy as Ahmed thought; it can be life-threatening. However, our electrician, Batti Sahab, rose to the occasion and volunteered. He had never exhibited what in northern India and Pakistan is called 'jigra' (courage), and we were all surprised to see this side of him. Batti Sahab was not a front-line guy, and on top of that, he didn't even know how to swim. But when he heard the plan was to use the breathing apparatus available on the ship to dive into the water and clean the propeller, it seemed like an adventure to him.

To be clear, the breathing apparatus found on ships has nothing to do with deep sea diving and is not designed for use under water; it's for fighting fires on board. There is only enough oxygen available for fifteen to twenty minutes, so Bada Sahab advised Batti Sahab to breathe slowly and not panic, so the oxygen could last longer. These words may seem obvious now, but in our context, they felt really scary.

The following morning, before Batti Sahab made his dive, Capt. Ram made a suggestion based on his experience on the boat the previous day. He asked Abdullah and some deck crew to clean the fore peak store—an area at the fo'c'sle used for general storage, which also has the anchor cable locker—and fill it up with seawater. With the extra weight at the front, the nose of the ship would go down and the rear would come up.

Now, this could have easily gone the other way, as we still had the cargo loaded and the weight was in the middle. If this proposed new weight distribution went too far, it could break the ship, but Capt. Ram had done his stability calculations well and knew this could be done temporarily, since we were anchored and not moving.

We all stood at the side of the deck as Batti Sahab went down to the boat. He had put the breathing apparatus on his back and the mask over his face, and a rope had been tied around his waist. For us on the deck, it was a nerve-wracking moment, and we couldn't even imagine how it was for Batti Sahab down there. We all continued to root for him, praying he'd be successful. Suddenly, we saw him jump into the water. There was no sign of him for a few seconds and we didn't know what to make of it. Though he was wearing a life jacket, the weight of the cylinders was so great that it just didn't help. The plan for him was never to dive deep into the water, and hence the life jacket. But he put his head under, using the breathing apparatus, and tried to swim closer to the hull of the ship and be able to see the propeller and marine growth around it.

Thankfully, we soon saw movement. The man holding the rope tied to Batti Sahab's waist was struggling to keep a grip on due to the strong current, while the weight of the breathing apparatus was pulling Batti Sahab down. He was giving everything he had to not only reach the propeller, but to survive.

After attempting the task for a while, the pirates realized its futility and called it off, thankfully before a tragedy happened. We finally breathed easy when Batti Sahab came back on board, safe and sound. He had earned my respect that day with his bravery, and I'm sure the others felt the same way.

But the pirates still didn't drop the idea of diving, and Bada Sahab had another brainwave—he suddenly remembered that one of the cadets was a state-level swimmer, and suggested that he dive instead of Batti Sahab. The pirates loved this idea, because it seemed to them that perhaps an adept swimmer would be able to accomplish the task without a life jacket and breathing apparatus. It's possible they weren't wrong; maybe he would be able to reach the propeller and remove the marine growth, if there was any to remove it in the first place.

The state-level swimmer in question was Senior Cadet Krishna. He was short but athletic, and when he took his T-shirt off, we could see the muscular cuts even after eight months of eating what we had, when we were all losing weight. We would ask him about it, and he would credit his training for swimming competitions, as well as 'toddy and fish fry', like his fellow cadet from Kerala, David, had said on his birthday back in April.

Krishna was a very bold guy who had lived a tough life back home, so he was not one to step back from a challenge easily. His ambition was to have a good career at sea and uplift his parents' standard of living.

Before going to bed that night, I asked him, 'Bro, are you sure about tomorrow?'

He replied, 'Bonge bhai, are we sure about anything here?' Then, he turned his face to the other side and we both closed our eyes.

The following morning, I woke up with a really bad stomach ache—so bad I was not even able to get out of bed. Bade and SK had to come and take me to the bridge. Among all the other issues confronting us, the one thing we were most scared of was falling sick. After all, we were hostages on a ship anchored in the sea, and if we fell sick, we were miles away from any kind of help. In these circumstances, we could only rely on our immune system to fight off the disease, with the help of the rudimentary first-aid facilities we had at our disposal on the ship.

When I reached the bridge, I was in no position to even speak. I was trying to have a word with Parjeet, who could possibly give me some medicines. He offered me a syrup bottle, and I instinctively checked the label for the expiry date, as we are all taught to do from childhood. The Second Officer said quickly, 'Look at the date and stay in pain, ignore the date and feel relief. In normal times, I wouldn't have given you this, but we left normal times back in Seychelles.' The pain was unbearable; I didn't have an option.

While I was on the bridge, a far worse crisis was emerging on deck. Krishna was preparing for his dive, but the scraping stick he had been handed was much smaller than the previous one, as the pirates assumed he'd dive and swim very close to the propeller. They were clearly not aware of the implausibility of this attempt or the risk of injury Krishna was facing.

Krishna reached the edge of the ship, from where he had to climb down to the boat. I can only imagine what was going on in the mind of that brave young cadet. I am certain that all of us were with him in spirit, but he was the one taking the leap of faith.

Before he took his first step down, Capt. Ram walked up to him and said, 'You can say no. If you don't want to go, just say no, and I will deal with what comes next.' The Captain had been against this idea from the beginning, but we all knew that it was beyond his control.

Krishna looked back at him and took a moment. 'I will do it, sir,' he said, and went down the ladder to the boat. He knew how crucial it was for our well-being on the ship.

After the first dive, he got back on the boat, where Capt. Ram and one of the pirates were keeping an eye on him. 'The current is too strong,' he told the Captain. He got into position to dive again. But at that moment, Abdullah, who was up on the deck holding the rope tied around Krishna's waist, saw a big fish appear out of nowhere, and raised an alarm. We saw it too—it was circling the diving boat. There wasn't a fin above the surface of the water; we only saw it because the water was clean and transparent. We were sure it wasn't a shark, but it could still be dangerous, and it was certainly huge. Everyone tried to guess what it could be. The pirates, too, were amazed to see it, and Camel Face even had the audacity to make the accusation, 'You bring fish to no go water.'

The whole operation stopped for a while as everyone waited for the fish to swim away. Minutes passed, but it was still there, circling the boat, disappearing for a little while and then suddenly reappearing out of nowhere. It was as if the sea gods were on our side that day and wanted this whole thing to stop. There was no way we were letting Krishna go into the water until it swam away. Eventually, the pirates had to cancel the plan for the day and try again the next day.

Krishna had described his experience underwater as the 'current slapping all over the place', which meant he just couldn't apply the force necessary to go deeper, and was pushed back every time he tried. He had some plans for how he would approach it the next time.

The next morning was day four of 'propeller cleaning', and we still hadn't got close to it. The crew members were exhausted; our energy levels were already low because of our food situation, and the operation went on from morning till sunset, which was, at least emotionally if not physically, taxing for most of us. I was feeling much better today and was on deck with the rest of the crew.

Bada Sahab and the pirates were hoping for success that day because the current looked calmer than previous days. But after hours of struggle, the outcome was no different. With each new idea, effort and initiative, the result remained the same—we couldn't reach the propeller, let alone clean it.

Finally, everybody agreed that the idea be dropped altogether. Krishna was pulled back on to the ship, having withstood the ordeal. We could see the mark the rope tied around his waist had left. He reported that he had been able to get a visual on the propeller, and didn't see much marine growth that could be affecting it.

And thus, the pirates' attempts to make us their accomplices in scaring and robbing people failed. We were still captives, but we didn't become hunters.

Bada Sahab's role in these goings-on did not sit well with the rest of us. His overly pacifying and accommodating behaviour towards the pirates at the cost of our well-being was not acceptable. As a result, most of us started giving him the cold shoulder. No one from the crew or cadets even extended greetings to him any more. In retrospect, I consider our behaviour to have been immature, but at the time, we didn't know any better. The senior officers dealt with him more maturely, although even they didn't include him in any important discussion, nor did they seek his counsel for anything related to the ship or the crew.

Some would say that our actions during those times were questionable, objectionable and nonsensical. I don't consider those adjectives unfair. But I am sure that in the deepest corners of our hearts, each of us was trying to survive our immense crisis the way we could. In the end, our will to survive and adapt was all that was going to count. Our nights were possibly the darkest because dawn was approaching. When was the sun going to rise, though?

11

Whims and Fancies of Our Captors

It was the middle of the day, with the sun shining bright in the sky. The memory of our shipmates being intimidated with guns on the shore was still fresh in our minds when our lives were put under threat again.

This time, it was an outraged Abdi maniacally pointing a gun at us. We couldn't figure out whether to be scared for our lives or just be stunned at the absurd behaviour of a man with a gun. We had been at the pirates' mercy for uncountable days now, but in that moment, we knew that if he chose to fire, or even accidentally shoot the gun in his rage, it would mean a loss of life.

There were multiple reasons for his rage. Omar had mentioned to me once that the pirates working on the ship only got paid once the ransom was received from the ship's owner. *RAK Afrikana* by now had been in Somalian waters much longer than anybody had anticipated. The shore supplies of the pirates were also dwindling as, with every passing day, their expenses to keep the ship there were increasing. We couldn't help them capture other ships and on top of all this the water level in the cargo hatch was contributing to the turmoil. As the days passed, we could see the water levels rising and just two hours of running the generator were falling short of sufficiently pumping out the water.

After the initial incident with Jafar holding the gun to my head, which I described at the start of this book, we had stopped going for sounding duty. But in time, I was entrusted with the task again. And sure enough, I had been noticing a rise in the water level inside the ballast tanks. My first guess was that the welding performed in Karachi had given way, as it had been a temporary fix. It could also be that a new hole had developed.

Initially, the amount of water coming in was not alarming, but we knew that either of these scenarios could lead to a major disaster if not addressed in time. I kept Capt. Ram and Parjeet updated twice a day on the sounding levels.

Capt. Ram didn't waste a moment and told the pirates about the impending crisis as the levels started increasing. As a counter measure to addressing the now-alarming situation, we installed an external portable pump. With limited diesel available, the pump ran for four hours every night, but every morning the water was back. It didn't take us long to realize that this was not the solution, because we were pumping out less water than what was coming in. Thus, to increase our pumping capacity, we requested the pirates to help and bring a second portable pump on board. Surprisingly, the second pump ran twenty-four hours every day as it needed very little diesel.

However, the problem was not getting resolved. Once again, somebody from the crew—we were certain it was Bada Sahab—secretly gave the pirates the idea that this hole could be closed and the water level would stop rising. This could be done with the help of the cement that we were carrying. Again, what a brilliant solution Bada Sahab had thought of!

This was not an easy or lasting fix. First, we needed to ascertain the source of the seepage. We knew where the original hole was, so we decided to look around the same area, which could only be accessed through the ballast tanks beneath the cargo deck. Seven or eight of us and a few pirates gathered on the deck to start the operation.

Before reaching the ballast tanks, we had in front of us the herculean task of moving a deck full of jumbo bags loaded with thousands of kilograms of cement. Each jumbo bag weighed a ton, and the cargo deck was around forty-five metres long and thirty-five metres wide, with a four-layer stacking of jumbo bags. You can imagine the number of bags we would have had to move to make our way through and reach the manhole leading to the ballast tanks.

Initially, we pumped out the water that was already inside. We went down to the cargo hold while three pirates remained on deck, examining and controlling us as if from a pedestal.

I was standing on one of the stacks. The four bags at the bottom of each stack were already inundated. Each jumbo bag, containing smaller bags of fifty kilograms each, was a metre high, which meant that the water had reached the four-metre mark in such a big space. We had to remove each fifty-kilogram bag with our hands, put on a rope sling or net, which the Bosun would then lift out of the hatch with the help of derricks (small crane-like structures to lift cargo) to make space for us to reach the cargo deck level. This would still have been okay, but because of the water, the cement inside most of the bags had gotten wet and become solid concrete, and the bags had got stuck together, so they could only be separated and removed using crowbars and hammers. Every time we stopped to separate the bags or to catch our breath, the water level would rise again. And from the pirates' perspective, it was one more day of burning diesel. They thought we could reach the hole in a day and box the area, and the problem would be solved. Now, who had the courage to explain to them that it was not that simple? I really wished Bada Sahab, who was giving them all these ideas, would just come and spend one day with us and realize what was happening, rather than just standing on the bridge wing and taking drags from his cigarette.

After around a week of arduous physical labour, we finally reached the manhole. That was when the pirates exhibited a baffling level of ignorance. Even though they were in the business of hijacking ships for ransom, they surprisingly did not know much about the structure of a ship. They only knew about the small skiffs they used. Therefore, more often than not, they compared those boats to vessels as big as ours. Under no circumstances was that a learned comparison.

Abdi was commanding the pirates on board at the time, and when we reached the manhole and talked about opening it, he lost his cool. The pirates had assumed that we were causing the water seepage intentionally. After looking at the manhole, Abdi, in his profound ignorance, believed opening it would let loose a fountain of seawater and the whole thing would be flooded. As far as he was concerned, we were trying to worsen the problem; he thought it was our nefarious plan to scare them away by flooding the ship, and this brought out the worst in him.

The ensuing argument between him and us became so intense that he ended up pushing me and others down with the tip of his gun and screaming, 'Stop, stop… ya stop, I shoot!' Chief Officer Baig and Second Officer Parjeet both tried to explain things to him, but he was not willing to listen to anything. So we just stood there, scared, because he held a gun over our heads as the seawater continued to make its way into the ship. We were wasting precious time because the pirates were misinformed.

Finally, after spending half a day convincing him, and some magic words from Bada Sahab, Abdi came to his senses and understood that the manhole was not at the bottom of the ship and had no direct access to seawater. We had won the argument but lost precious time dealing with his ignorance. In those few hours, the water had seeped in again, and had to be pumped out.

After the failed first attempt, this time we did open the manhole. Again, one of the pirates hurried us to get inside the ballast tank. We had to tell him that the tank had been closed for all these months and there was no oxygen in it, so we would have to wait for the space to get ventilated. That, naturally, didn't make him happy. Capt. Ram ensured Bada Sahab remained on deck and was involved in the proceedings to make the pirates understand, because they seemed to be listening to him.

The ballast tanks are not exactly a convenient space to move through; only crew members used to such movements in their safety gear can navigate them skilfully. Yet, in a further display of his ignorance, Abdi remained adamant that he would not let us go alone inside, because he was still convinced that we were making the problem worse. A whole lot of the pirates present there didn't trust us at all; they wanted to take their guns along into the narrow space.

Somehow, with the help of Bada Sahab, we convinced them that taking guns inside was impractical and extremely dangerous for two reasons—one, because the ballast tanks were structurally designed in a way that the pirates wouldn't be able to move so easily through the space with guns in their hands, and two, because the tank space was dark and an accidental or panicked shot could injure or kill anyone inside, and even damage the hull further.

When the argument was settled and our crew was prepping to climb down, surprisingly, none of the pirates was willing to go inside. Parjeet and an oiler, wearing full safety gear and holding a torch, went down and waited for someone from the pirates to join them. After much debate and more lost time, Abshir from the pirates volunteered—the shortest and one of the youngest among them, who had been on the bridge during the crossfire with the chopper and whose gun had jammed.

Parjeet led them down to find the source of the seepage, but no one could see anything. To our good fortune, the sound of water gushing in was clear, and we had a witness from the pirates' side who heard it too but couldn't spot it. This meant the hole was at a place where nothing could be done from the inside; it had to be welded at the dock.

But the pirates were still suspicious and unconvinced, and that made it more difficult to explain that the ship could not be fixed the way their small boats could be. After a point, we gave up on the idea of reasoning with them.

Finally, when Abdi was convinced that there was no way to fix the leak, he came up with an idea that was even more fantastical than plugging the leak with cement—he asked us to arrange for a tarpaulin sheet and cover the whole side of the ship from where the seawater was entering. The moment he said it, we realized that we were in for another laborious, physically daunting task. Abdi, of course, had not figured out the exact details of how to execute it, but it was in his head, and Abdullah the Bosun had to execute it.

Abdullah laid out a plan. Then, he took out the thickest material he could find and suggested putting it over the bow of the ship and pulling it from both sides. We agreed to the plan; there was not much we could say to sway the pirates from another fool's errand.

The Bosun was aware that it was a tricky task, so he handpicked specific members of the crew based on their capabilities, which he had learnt over the long hours he spent working with them. Bade and I were part of this team of ten, including Abdullah himself, and we gathered on the deck.

Abdullah casually mentioned to me, 'You haven't rested in days, and you still have the energy …'

I replied, 'I lost my sleep nine months ago, boss.'

He looked at me, smiled and said, 'Let's tie this diaper to the ship.'

We had made our preparations and were about to start the operation when Abdi told us we had to first address another issue that needed immediate attention. 'You first do this, and then that,' he commanded. So, Operation Tarpaulin was put on hold, and we moved to another side of the ship.

One of the pirates' boats—ironically, the same one they had used to hijack us—had had an engine failure, so we had tied it to the aft of our ship. But thanks to the heavy waves, its hull had developed a crack. At this moment, when the waves were picking up, the boat was about a foot below the surface of the water, and only thanks to Abdullah's tight knot was it still hanging on to the aft railing. The pirates had done one smart thing, taken out the engine, so that only the fibre hull remained. Our task now was to bring the boat to the deck.

When this series of tasks had started, we did not mind engaging in the physical activity, because it was a change from months of inactivity. But now, with the seemingly never-ending cycle of tasks, that feeling had gone away. We just wanted all of it to be over. At one point, while pulling the boat up, I thought of just cutting the rope and letting it sink. At least that would take one task off our hands. But that would have meant risking all our lives, so I kept pulling the boat up.

In the middle of our struggles to pull the rope up against the wild waves, it began to rain. Every time we got a good grip, the waves pushed the boat back down, which dragged us to the edge. We were wearing safety gloves, but they were not much use, because the pirates had snatched away our new gloves and left us with old, worn-out ones. Our fingers were wounded, and the lack of even basic first-aid worried us.

While Abdullah held the rope tied to the railing, even with our bruised palms and fingers, we managed to bring the boat close enough to the derrick hook. The next challenge was to hook the boat, for which somebody needed to go down into the water. It was dangerous, and the pirates naturally expected us to take the risk. But this time, we put our foot down and refused to risk our lives. We had reached an impasse.

To our surprise, one of the pirates volunteered for the task. We prepped him properly for the dive, mostly out of self-preservation, because we didn't want any retaliation if anything happened to him. With a rope tied around his waist, he climbed down. It was dark and I could barely see him in the torchlight. However, he swiftly dove in and hooked the boat, and left us admiring his bravery, even if begrudgingly.

At the other end, Abdullah was handling the controls of the derrick while Hassan, the pirate boat captain, signalled from the deck. Once on the deck level, the boat had to be positioned between two containers. The task needed efficient communication and signalling between the two men, but that never happened. The boat got severely damaged during the operation; its front side was completely crushed. As seafarers, the apathy and recklessness of the pirates was a troubling sight for us. 'I hope they don't do the same to our ship,' I said quietly to Abdullah. 'I fear the same,' he replied.

The unnerving realization dawned on us that the fate of our vessel and our lives was in the hands of incompetent amateurs.

Nevertheless, we spent the whole night bringing the boat to the deck. It was to be repaired later by the pirates themselves. But that was not the end of our night, because Operation Tarpaulin still awaited us.

We hadn't taken a break in a long time, and some of us were too tired to start another physically demanding task. The futility of the tasks also dampened our spirits; most of the time, we weren't sure if whatever we were doing was making any difference.

And yet, later that night, we started lowering the tarpaulin. The only thing in our favour was that it had stopped raining. Three crew members each on either side of the deck started pulling it up. We were executing the whole operation on a whim, with no precise calculations. Considering the size of the ship and the tarpaulin, we didn't even know how much rope we'd need. We had already used our last reels of rope. In addition, the containers on the starboard side became an obstruction for us while pulling the tarpaulin closer to the ship. Moreover, we were sure the pirates had not considered the marine growth at the bottom of the ship, and if it was immense, it might tear the tarpaulin, and the whole manoeuvre would be for nothing.

With all these doubts swirling in our minds, our bodies exhausted and our spirits shackled, we pulled and pulled until our palms started to bleed. But we successfully covered a large part of the ship with the tarpaulin and hoped it would stop the water from seeping in. In those desperate times, hope was all we had.

In the middle of all this activity, some of the crew members, me included, were scared of the worst-case scenario: that our ship would capsize. Because of the water seepage on the starboard side and the heavy waves, we were rolling about four to five degrees on that side. I remember a moment on the bridge when Capt. Ram was doing the calculations for the stability of the ship with Parjeet. The readings were not good. Capt. Ram looked at me and asked, 'Are you scared?' I couldn't utter a word, so I just nodded. 'As long as I am here, I won't let anything happen to the ship,' he added with wink. His words gave me confidence.

There had not been much communication between the men at work on the cargo deck and our Captain. We were in a tough spot, and I am certain the Captain was equally worried. But every time we saw him around, he would be calm and composed, like a true leader. Later, when our ordeal eventually got over, we learnt that there was one thing most crew members didn't have a clue about, and had we known, our worries would have abated a bit.

You see, sometime during the fiasco, Capt. Ram had asked to move some of the cargo towards the starboard side. His goal was to cause just enough rolling of the ship (the tilting of the port and starboard along the ship's longitudinal axis) to scare the pirates, and he had achieved it. After we got the tarpaulin on, the pirate on the monkey island experienced the worst of the body roll, and remained terrified. Unfortunately, we experienced it too in our accommodation, and that scared us because we had no idea at the time that this was a deliberate ploy on the Captain's part to intimidate the pirates in the hope that this would speed up the ransom negotiations.

From start to end, this whole episode lasted a couple of weeks, and we accomplished some far-fetched tasks in an attempt to make our days a little safer and more harmonious. We didn't know what the future held for us; all we could do was live and survive each day, following the whims and fancies of our captors.

Perhaps the crises we were now facing were a sign that everything was finally falling apart. Our ship was in bad shape, our morale had plummeted and our physical strength was weakening with each passing day. Yet, we were no closer to emancipation.

Eventually, to make things worse for us, the two gigantic tasks we had accomplished turned out to be in vain—the pirates' boat sank when they put it back in the water after they had finished repairing it, and the tarpaulin didn't stop the water from seeping in.

Abdi and his boss Ahmed then started conducting rounds of this ship, and exploring places they had not been to until now. They wanted to cross-check and ensure we were not making all these things up.

They didn't understand that the mere thought of our ship sinking petrified us. On one side, there was endless open ocean, and on the other, three miles away, an unknown land with unknown dangers. We had nowhere to go.

With these lingering worries on our minds, our lives as captives on our now-dead ship went on.

12

Bloody T-Shirt

We were now entering our tenth month in captivity. The tarpaulin still covered the bottom of the ship, but seawater continued to seep in, and the pirates' damaged boat rested on our cargo deck.

The hijacking had stretched much longer than any of us had expected, including the pirates. They, too, were exhibiting the after-effects of the delay, as with every passing day, they grew desperate, frustrated and haphazardly violent. The number of pirates keeping an eye on us had reduced substantially. Now, they were behaving erratically. The guys on board were not getting paid at all because of the delayed negotiations, and they were not getting relievers easily as not too many wanted to come back to our ship. Instead, they wanted to stick to newly arrived ships, where supplies and conditions were much better. And above all, the number one reason for their unwillingness to come back was that the other ships were not sinking.

Things had gone back to being calm, so we didn't anticipate that yet another figurative storm was about to hit us, and this would be the hardest yet. We occupied ourselves in our daily routines, pumping out seawater in the daytime and filling up freshwater at night. Both were equally important for our survival.

Then one morning, we again saw an unusual flurry of activity on our ship. A lot of people were suddenly on board. Generally, we would be informed beforehand of such movements, but there had been no warning this time, or any kind of chatter about an activity that necessitated new people to come on the ship. We had barely gotten out of our beds when we were all summoned on the deck.

We gathered there in a state of frenzy, and I observed some different faces around, including those whom we hadn't seen in a while, like Abdi, Ahmed the boss and Tarjuman. All their countenances seemed different that morning.

As soon as everybody had gathered on the deck, they divided us into groups of four to five individuals. All the cadets and crew members remained on deck, while they sent the senior officers to the bridge. The Chief Cook was not around; he had not been keeping well.

After a while, the groups on the deck were pushed towards different sections of the ship. Abdullah, Bade and I were sent to the anchor room in the forward section of the ship, along with Azizi Makame, 'Uncle', who was part of the crew as an able seaman, or A/B. He was an amazing personality. He was the oldest person on board, and we cadets had nicknamed him that. To us, he was like the wrestler Hulk Hogan—old but muscular. He might not have been the quickest guy, but in terms of strength, he could've given anyone a run for their money.

The most peculiar memory I have of Uncle is the way he always said, 'That's OK, that's all right' to everything. Like the rest of the crew, he also hailed from Tanzania, and his knowledge of English was limited, so he would always respond using this phrase. Uncle had been a seafarer since his teenage years, and everything about him suggested a long career at sea. With age, he had developed noticeably hunched shoulders, which made him look short, since he wasn't very tall anyway, but his arms and biceps were still tough. The day he would be chipping (removing rust from steel) on deck, you could easily see his veins protruding.

His dedication to work was commendable; he would never say no to it, regardless of what time of day it was. I remember, once, in the middle of the night, I knocked on his door to inform him to be on stand-by for anchor station. We had had a long, tiring day, and it wasn't even his turn at anchor station. Still, within a few minutes, he was fully geared up for work. He didn't even bother to ask 'what' or 'why'; he just got ready to work, as always.

So, in the moment, the four of us—Abdullah, Uncle, Bade and I—were locked inside the forward mast store, which was the same place where the seawater had been filled up to bring the nose down when we were trying to scrape the propeller. It had filled up quickly enough, but draining the water had been a never-ending process, and the memory was still very fresh.

Many crucial tools required to operate the ship were stored in this room. And everything stored there, including the vital anchor cable locker, was made of materials extremely prone to corrosion, so we couldn't afford to leave even a drop of seawater in the compartment. It had been a long and tedious job to dry it out, made worse by the heat and humidity in the compartment. In our circumstances, it had taken us four days to remove the water, using buckets and even garbage scoops. We had dried out the remaining drops with cloth, ensuring no moisture was left behind. It was backbreaking work, but we had made the space dry.

Now, we were back in there, and the air once again was hot, humid and morbid. Bade and I were sitting on the floor, while Abdullah was pacing the room, when he saw a roll of rope. These things always interested the Bosun, and he started checking it out for its strands and splicing, while Uncle quietly prayed in a corner. We were completely clueless about what was happening outside, until we heard that most dreaded sound. Gunshots. All we could do was hope nobody had been hurt, because the door was locked from the outside.

Some time later, we heard somebody opening the lock. Two pirates came in, and grabbed me and Bade by our collars and hurled us out on the deck. Still confused and scared, we stood on deck while Abdullah and Uncle remained inside.

The pirates made us stand facing the fo'c'sle, with our backs towards the bridge. One of them then pushed us to the ground and made us kneel, with our hands behind our heads. Were we going to be the target for the next set of gunshots? At the back of my mind, I had always had a faint idea that this might happen, sooner or later. But soon, we realized it wasn't that time yet, as Mohammed, the storekeeper, approached us briskly, pointing to the pump room. He threw something on the floor in front of us, then went and stood behind us.

It was a T-shirt, and I knew to whom it belonged—my batchmate SK. I had seen him wearing it a while ago on the deck, and while it had been yellow then, now, it was crimson red. I was still trying to make sense of it when Mohammed said the dreadful words, 'This your friend blood. Your company no pay, we kill everyone now.'

In an instant, everything went still for me. No thoughts, nothing whatsoever. Not even reflexes. I didn't know how to react to the knowledge that one of us, my friend and batchmate, had been mercilessly killed by the pirates.

The sun was at our backs, and I could see my shadow, as well as that of the pirate standing behind me. A few seconds later, I saw the shadow of his gun too, as he pulled it up and rested it against the back of my head. The coldness of death seemed to seep into me from the metal of the barrel. They had already killed one, and now, my time was up. My eyes were welling up with tears, so I closed them. I could feel my heart pumping at a high rate, and going even faster. Everything else went silent, and I could only hear my heartbeat. Then, I heard more gunshots, and my body shivered in shock, thinking this was the end.

But it wasn't. When the unthinkable didn't happen, I opened my eyes and saw the pirate's shadow moving away. It took a few seconds for my whole body to respond, starting with a pain in my knees, which were pressing against the hot deck floor. My mind registered that the immediate threat was gone, and I had been spared. My body, however, took time to recover. Even though the pirate was gone, I couldn't move a muscle. Bade and I just shared a glance, and then stared into the abyss. No words were uttered. Our bodies felt cramped from head to toe.

Afterwards, we were asked to get up and again gather on the main deck. If the pirates were on a killing spree, why hadn't they shot me? What had I done to be spared while SK was shot to death? Was the worst of it over? Perhaps the pirates had satisfied their bloodlust and were done for the day.

With all these thoughts running in my mind, I reached the cargo hold near our accommodation, and that's when I saw SK, alive and standing bare-chested. Needless to say, that was a great relief. Later, we learnt that the blood on the T-shirt had come from a goat the pirates had brought in earlier that day. It was yet another attempt at scaremongering, because they had shown the same T-shirt to Capt. Ram and the officers on the bridge. Apparently, the pirates had tied the Captain to his chair on the bridge deck and kept him there throughout their drama.

I thought we had seen enough for one day, but I was wrong. In a few minutes, the scene on the deck got ghastlier, as each one of the cadets and crew was made to kneel on top of the cargo hatch. The senior officers were brought down from the bridge too, their hands were tied and they were forced to lie on their stomachs on the deck floor. The cargo net opened in front of them while the hook of the crane hung over their heads.

'We will put you in this net and throw you in the water,' one of the pirates announced. I spotted Abdallah Saidi, our able seaman, standing next to the crane with a gun pointed at him. Saidi was a short, chubby guy, who was quick and efficient at any kind of deck work. He was one of the most polite and humble persons on board and always followed instructions without any question. But now, with the gun pointed at his head, the fear on his face was obvious. If the pirates followed through on their words, he would've been forced to operate the crane that dumped his crewmates into the sea. The weight he must've felt was unimaginable.

The pirates wanted immediate ransom payment, and figured that if they upped the threat level through violence, it would pressure the owner into accepting their demands quicker. But we had no information about the negotiations, nor did we know if we had done something in particular to enrage them.

As I've said before, the pirates had assumed we were letting seawater into the ship on purpose, as well as hiding fuel. The only rationale behind this new, violent behaviour seemed to be that they were trying to break our spirits, like they had tried with our people on the shore. They wanted us to plead with the owner, which they had made Capt. Ram do on the shore at gunpoint. But even after all these months, our spirit was intact. The Captain was as strong as he had been at the beginning of our ordeal. If they were doing this to break our morale as a group, it wasn't really working.

But within a group, there are always individuals who are weaker-willed than the others. The pirates probably saw themselves as big cats hunting wildebeest, and even though our herd was strong, they were trying to find the weakest member. And they did.

One pirate started yelling at Third Officer Kuldeep, who was kneeling with us on the cargo hatch cover. The pirate asked him to come down, and when he didn't, he grabbed his arm and pulled him down. Kuldeep barely managed to land on his feet. He could have been hurt, but what lay for him ahead was far more horrendous—the sight shook not just him, but most of us as well.

Two pirates held him up with great force and took him towards the deck railing. Before anyone could react, they picked him up by his arms and legs and brought him parallel to the railing. I could feel a chill run down my spine—they were going to throw him overboard.

Kuldeep was a six-foot-tall man, who was now crying like a baby and screaming for help, desperate to get away from their grasp of death. For some reason, he kept asking for their forgiveness, yelling, 'I am sorry, let me go!'

We all stood and watched, helpless and powerless. This time, even Bada Sahab was on the ground with his hands tied behind his back. They had found a few tons of diesel in the emergency generator tank, which flipped their lids, and they came to the conclusion that he had been hiding it from them. That's when Bada Sahab finally realized that these people couldn't be trusted at all. We could see this realization in his eyes as he spoke to Capt. Ram, who was lying next to him.

There is an Urdu saying, '*Der aaye, durust aaye*', for which the English equivalent is 'Better late than never'. But the 'durust' in the Urdu saying means well-being, and as Bada Sahab was finding out, our well-being was still not guaranteed. Our ordeal was far from over.

13

'Save Ship, Save Lives'

Our world had suddenly gone soundless, motionless and morbid. One of us was about to be thrown overboard. As Kuldeep hung in the air, awaiting his fate, we were there with him in spirit, but we could only imagine the extent of horror he must have been feeling. I came back to my senses with the sound of the Third Officer hitting the deck floor, still alive.

He lay on the ground, barely moving, his hands over his face. For some reason, the pirates had spared him too. He was distraught, shattered and scarred, but alive. We were relieved.

He continued to lie still for some time, crying. I am not sure if he would ever find the strength in his heart to come to terms with what had happened. While he cried his heart out, we stood frozen, without a peep. For us, the incident had brought us out of whatever slumber we had left in us. Any one of us could have been in his place. Most of us didn't even know how we would react if it had been us instead of him.

Thankfully, the moment had not ended in tragedy. We wanted to go to our brother-in-arms and assist him in whatever way we could, but the pirates were still not done with us. With each passing minute, we were subjected to a new form of torture. Things had been going more and more awry for us every month since September.

We were still gathering our scattered thoughts when the pirates pushed us towards the next torture. Once again, they became obsessed with the idea of plugging the leak on the ship. They asked us to get inside the cargo hatch and threatened to kill us one by one if we didn't stop the seepage. They were still under the impression that we had intentionally let seawater in.

From the deck, Ahmed and Abdi threatened us to 'remove as much bag as you want, find another place and stop water'. If we didn't succeed, they would leave all the crew inside the lower cargo hold and lock every exit.

There we were, once again, going through the same back-breaking activity as a few weeks ago. We cadets got inside the hatch, picked up our crowbars and started taking out the cement bags. Abdullah was still held at the derrick operating station, and we could see some officers standing on the upper deck of the cargo hold (our cargo holds were separated into two levels—the upper level was called the weather deck and the lower level the tween deck. So the *RAK Afrikana* was a tween-decker general cargo ship). The other officers, including Capt. Ram, stood on the tween deck. I couldn't see them as I was way down below, but could hear them all, including Abdi.

After a while, I heard yelling from the tween deck. Everyone was pointing in a particular direction and shouting;

something had gone wrong again. Me and some other cadets who were near the ladder to the tween deck immediately started climbing. At some distance, we saw Capt. Ram lying on the ground while two pirates pointed their guns at him, ready to fire. Parjeet was massaging the Captain's feet, but the latter was not moving. The only word out of my mouth was 'fuck'; my mind agreed, 'We are fucked.'

We were still a fair bit away from the scene, moving slowly, had no clue what had happened, and were trying to gauge what was going on. We had learnt that we could never rush towards the pirates, no matter what, as they might just open fire without understanding or thinking.

Capt. Ram was still not moving. Parjeet made eye contact with us and called out, '*Jaldi aao* (Come quick).' Were we going to lose him? The Captain was the anchor that had kept us all grounded and in high spirits all along. Losing him was unimaginable.

It was undeniable that the Captain was in bad shape. Bada Sahab, sitting on the hatch cover on the main deck, hollered at the Bosun. The Captain needed immediate medical attention; we had to get him out of the tween deck and into open air. The pirates finally realized this was serious, and they did what they were best at in such situations—left us to it.

Parjeet quickly asked a senior cadet to go to the ship's hospital and get the stretcher. I, too, ran to Abdullah and asked him to prepare ropes so we could lift the Captain out of the cargo hold. He suggested using the derrick, but the pirates' supply of fuel for that day had not arrived yet, so the generator could not be switched on, and it was too windy, so there was a high chance of the stretcher swinging and maybe banging against the cargo bulkhead, which could hurt Capt. Ram more.

Abdullah quickly told two of his deck crew to get ropes from the store, which was locked as the pirates had their weapons there. We had no time to explain to the pirates what we wanted, so I told Abdullah, 'Boss, remember those ropes we saw in the forward mast store?' He liked the idea and said, 'Yes, get them quick, I'll make it work.'

As I came back, even the stretcher had arrived. The Second Officer and the other cadets had moved the Captain closer to where the stretcher would be lowered, and once Abdullah was confident about the ropes, he sat on the edge of the cargo hatch cover with one leg inside, and released it down, with the welder, Luca Baba, holding the other side. Parjeet and my fellow cadets carefully placed Capt. Ram on the stretcher and secured him in. Abdullah had left another piece of rope hanging from the stretcher that anyone below could hold to control the swing while he and Luca Baba lifted it up. This was done slowly and carefully, and we managed to get Capt. Ram up to the main deck.

The ship's hospital was one floor below the bridge on the same level as the Captain's and other officers' cabins, in the accommodation section. Senior cadets Sandeep and David manoeuvred the stretcher with great precision, right from entering the accommodation, passing by the officers' mess room and climbing the stairs to the upper levels, so that the Captain's head didn't hit anything on the way up. We noticed that Capt. Ram's eyes were now wide open, and he was looking around in confusion. We didn't know whether his other senses were working or not, but he was definitely silent as we reached the hospital.

Now the pirates came back on the scene and told us to stop crowding the space. They thought since the Captain was in the hospital, everything was fine, and started pressuring some of us to go down to the mess rooms. But we hesitated, and for the first time, they saw our resistance.

Honestly, in that moment, if there was a little aggression from them, there would have been a battle. All of us, especially the cadets, were ready to take them on. None of us spoke, but our emotions were showing prominently on our faces and in our body language. Hence, the pirates took a step back. One of them ran down and came back with Abdi and Ahmed.

Capt. Ram was now moved to the bed. He managed to lift his right hand up with great difficulty and signalled to Parjeet to come closer. Then, he told him something, but it was inaudible, so Parjeet bent down to listen and the Captain whispered it in his ear. Then he closed his eyes.

Parjeet convinced us to go back to the mess rooms, where the rest of the officers had gone already. Only three people stayed behind—Parjeet, Senior Cadet Sandeep and Bada Sahab. From the pirates' side too, only Ahmed and Abdi remained.

All of us sat in the dark in the officers' mess room, the only source of light being the aft deck opening at the end of the galley. After a few minutes, Chief Officer Ali Baig and Second Engineer Mir Balach started talking about what was going on upstairs. They were sitting at a distance from us and almost whispering, but we could hear them. And it made sense why Baig wanted to be discreet about it.

Standard protocol dictates that in the event of the Captain becoming indisposed, the Chief Officer takes command of the ship. But Baig was clearly in a very negative state of mind and had already started speculating about worst-case scenarios. He repeatedly mentioned the repercussions of something happening to Capt. Ram, and how it would affect everyone on the ship.

We had no issue that he was talking about the worst outcomes. All of us were aware of the circumstances and knew what lay in store for us. But we took issue with him on one point—we were still not willing to accept losing Capt. Ram. There was no update on his condition, and we were angry, desperate and restless.

Sentiments started piling up, and we cadets spoke among ourselves about what was on our minds. If anything happened to the Captain, we knew we would revolt and take those bloody pirates down. Even before this episode, occasionally, the thought of forcefully taking control of the ship had occurred to us. At times, we had played the scenarios out in our minds, such as how we could take one pirate hostage, get a hold of his gun and move to the others. We never acted on those thoughts because of the risk they entailed—if we made one wrong move, it could cost lives. But now, it was time. We knew if anything happened to Capt. Ram, it would be the end for us too. And if the end was nigh, might as well go down fighting.

Finally, about an hour and a half after we had come down from the hospital, Parjeet and Sandeep brought us an update: 'The Captain is stable now.' The words had an immediate calming effect on all of us, including Baig. 'I knew it! *Fighting spirit hai unn mein* (He has a fighting spirit)!' he beamed.

Later, we learnt that Capt. Ram had had a stroke. In an earlier conversation with him, he had mentioned that he had been feeling a little uneasy, with some numbness in his left arm. He ignored the symptoms, assuming they had appeared due to not having regular medication or nutritious food. Gradually, he had started feeling better, and even though he had lost a lot of strength in his left arm, in time, it started coming back. He had also ignored the issue because he had bigger problems to deal with.

That's what Capt. Ram was like—no matter his own condition, he refused to take anybody's help. 'I can't always depend on somebody helping me,' he'd say. We'd offer to help him when he struggled to wear his boiler suit, but he never agreed. Even while climbing the stairs to the bridge, he never took the support of the handrails.

Two days after the stroke, I accompanied the Captain back to the bridge. Naturally, he wasn't as agile going up the stairs as before, and was taking the support of the handrails this time. I was behind him and offered my assistance, but sure enough, he refused it. It was the most impressive trait of his personality—men like him set an example for self-reliance, pride and honour.

A few days later, I asked Parjeet, 'Sir, what did the Captain say in your ear that evening at the hospital despite his frail condition?'

Parjeet looked at me, smiled and said, 'Tell the boys, "Save ship, save lives."'

14

Camaraderie and Brotherhood

After tormenting us with more threats of life and putting us under immense pressure and stress, which led to the ensuing health crisis of Capt. Ram, the pirates seemed to retreat. Perhaps they found our cumulative will too strong to break.

For weeks after the Captain's stroke, there was another abominable lull on the ship. The pirates ceased all communication, even when we enquired about medical supplies. The number of pirates on board further reduced, till there were only four or five of them to keep an eye on two dozen of us. Even Bada Sahab was firmly back on our side, having realized that their 'promises' were just empty words meant to take advantage of the situation.

Through weeks of silence, we started getting back to our mundane, seemingly purposeless existence. At least that's how most of us felt. The only positive sign for us was that we could see Capt. Ram getting his strength back with each passing day. He was bringing himself into shape out of sheer willpower, because sitting idle in a corner was an absolutely disagreeable thought for him. We were aware that he was still far from his usual self, but slowly and steadily, he was on his way to recovery.

As far as our material needs were concerned, we and our ship were all in bad shape. But we still continued to help our brother sailors on the nearby ships by giving them daily freshwater by reducing our share. The production had also come down because the generator run time was also reduced, but we had to do our best for our own crew and the others struggling around us. I am sure the pirates would have never mentioned to the other ship where the freshwater was coming from and must have shown it was them being merciful to the crew. But we didn't care about credit, as long as we helped ease somebody else's misery. For us food was scarce, and even the frozen food items had to be discarded now as the generator's run time had been further reduced to only one and a half hours. Times, indeed, were getting tougher and more desperate with each passing day, but we had learnt to live in these conditions by now.

It was now February 2011, and very soon it would be one whole year in the Somali pirates' captivity. And since they had upped the ante in the last five months, in our heads we were like, 'What can be worse than this?' What was left to happen for us to break completely and give in to the thought that we would never see freedom or get back home to our families?

From the pirates' vantage point, they had tried every trick to subdue us and break our spirits—scaring, intimidating, making us feel vulnerable. They had succeeded to an extent.

We hadn't yet revolted, as we had thought of doing a few weeks ago. However, it was not enough for them. At the end of the day, they had hoped to make a lot of money from hijacking us, but that had not happened. So, until that point, it had been a bad investment for them.

The most pertinent question on our minds was how the pirates would react, now that they were disastrously cornered. We couldn't help but ponder the what-ifs. They might start acting even more violently in their desperation and frustration. If maintaining the status quo on the ship was difficult, they could take us to the shore, within their national borders (we were anchored within Somalia's maritime boundary, which for any country is twelve to fifteen nautical miles from land). Our worst fear was that they would kill one or more of us.

There were also thoughts about what would happen if they just abandoned us once the ransom was paid. One fine day, all of them could just get off the ship into their small boats and leave. What would happen to us then? We were neither in a position to survive for long without supplies, nor could we move our ship. The closest port, Mombasa in Kenya, was too far in our circumstances, as there was no fuel and not enough food for us to survive. And even if we theoretically starved and made it there, we would first have to get out of here, which meant we would need a powered engine—and ours was not an option. If we did somehow manage to leave these waters, there would always be the risk of getting hijacked by another group operating in the region. The best-case scenario that all of us, including the pirates, had been hoping for was that the owner would pay the ransom. But what about after that? Would they send another ship to tow us? That could be a risky undertaking.

And so, between all these thoughts, our lives remained in suspended animation. The pirates being in a bit of a retreat meant most of us now had the freedom to roam around the ship without supervision, and we the cadets were allowed to bring out our books and study. Crew members entertained themselves by playing cards, which Abdullah had warned them against, because he believed they would end up fighting each other over a game. They had done so earlier, and torn up the cards too, but glued the cards back together and continued to play.

We did chores on different parts of the ship during the day, and at night we would retreat to our sleeping arrangements in the mess room. Chief Officer Baig and the engineers followed in the footsteps of Bada Sahab and highlighted their back-pain issues, and after multiple requests were allowed to go back to sleeping in their cabins. Third Officer Kuldeep, after the horrific threat to his life the other day, had gone numb. We tried to cheer him up now and then, but the incident had clearly taken its toll on him. When we had run out of salt six months ago, he had picked up a hobby of trying to make salt by evaporating seawater on a hot plate. But now, he gave that up too.

One morning, I came across Abdullah working on a large fish net and a bucket. Out of curiosity, I asked if he needed help, but he politely refused. Our Bosun was a perfectionist when it came to things like these, and only took assistance from crew members who he really knew could help him. It would take time, but the thing would come out perfect.

I asked, 'What do you plan to do with this?'

Abdullah paused, looked at me and realized I wasn't about to go away. So, he said, 'Get me my cigarette and you can help me.' The idea was to put the net at the bottom of the sea and catch crabs.

'You seem happier than usual,' I told him, since this had become a rare occurrence. I was worried Abdullah had also made peace that he wasn't getting back home anytime soon.

But he replied with tears in his eyes. 'The last time I got to call my wife from the monkey island, with the Captain and Tarjuman, I finally heard my newborn daughter's voice. Every time I feel low I think about that day and get strength from it to last a few days longer here,' he said.

When he broke the news to me, I just hugged and congratulated him. The ship's crew felt great happiness for each other in such moments.

We strolled around for a bit and reached the deck, where our morning tea was being prepared on a makeshift stove. I took my cup and climbed to the bridge deck. A couple of other cadets were with me, while some others were studying or doing chart work. It was a bright day, and appeared to be quiet and uneventful. In fact, there had been weeks of inaction, so in my mind, something was about to happen; it was due any day now.

Sure enough, it was then that I saw Jafar talking to Capt. Ram in the chart room and making a peculiar gesture. I could discern that he was talking about somebody coming to the ship, and he looked excited. However, Capt. Ram and the rest of us had all stopped paying attention to any such piece of news. The Captain's only query was if we were getting medicines, and to that Jafar had no response.

By that afternoon, we saw Tarjuman approaching in a boat, climbing the ladder to the ship and sitting on the deck, panting, reminiscent of the first time he had boarded the ship ten months ago. He was wearing his usual attire of a vest and black tights. The funny thing was that even after all these months, out of all the pirates, only his clothes looked too small; everyone else's appeared oversized.

Tarjuman went straight to the bridge to meet Capt. Ram. This was his first time alone on board since the bloody T-shirt incident. His first words to Capt. Ram were: 'My mother is very sick, so I did not call you so many days.'

Tarjuman was carrying some papers in a plastic bag, and I could overhear some of the conversation between him and Capt. Ram. 'Good news, need answers!' Tarjuman said in an excited tone. I assumed he would be talking about updates on fuel, supplies, etc., so I didn't pay any more attention. But soon after, the Captain came out of the chart room and summoned everyone to the bridge. Only Chief Cook Muhammed was exempted because he had not been keeping well and was resting in the crew mess room.

So here we were, gathered at the bridge again. Some of us were even scared—lately, every time we had been called together, it had turned out to be an unpleasant experience.

Capt. Ram explained to us what Tarjuman was asking for—he had a list that contained three questions for each of us to answer. The pirates would send the answers to the ship owner, who would relay the information to our families. The whole process was intended to send them assurance that the pirates had not killed any of us yet. Providing proof of life in such a manner was surreal.

At the same time, this strange demand also gave us back some hope. We assumed that perhaps it was the first step to getting our freedom back. Maybe the negotiations had moved forward and a settlement had already been reached. If that was the case, it was only a matter of time before we were put out of our misery.

We were all together in probably the darkest time of our lives, and hope is what we needed to sail through. The whole ship had become like one large family, which was all the more obvious when we sat answering questions about our homes and families. The questions had definitely been sent by people who knew us, and although we had talked about our personal lives before, in pairs or small groups, that afternoon, for the first time, we shared our personal lives in front of the whole crew, and that only seemed to enhance our camaraderie. Talking about our homes and families was an emotional undertaking, and the sublimity of the whole episode was not lost on me, or anybody else present.

Of course, the bonding also included making fun of each other. One of the cadets was asked the name of one of his grandfathers, and he was confused between 'Mangeram' and 'Mangelal'. It was understandable, since in our part of the world, one barely ever used their grandparents' names to address them or talk about them. Nevertheless, we had some fun at his expense.

Another cadet was asked to write his niece's name. He complained that the niece hadn't even been born when he had boarded the ship, to which Capt. Ram replied with a laugh, '*Abe saale* (You fool), born in front of you or not, the family must have told you what name they gave her!'

The first two questions for me were to name both my uncles who lived in Pilani, and the answers—Gandhi Baba and Munna Chacha—gave the others no cause for mirth. But the third question brought the ribbing on to me, because I had to write the name of a restaurant from my neighbourhood when I was growing up in Muscat.

'It is only natural that you have to answer that!' said one of my friends. 'They know that you won't forget a food place!' said another.

Yes, yes, I was fond of food, so the joke was on me. I was quite sure these questions were sent by my father, especially the last one. That made me smile. Such small moments played a very important role in keeping our hopes high.

After all the humour and even a few tears, everyone handed over their answers to Tarjuman.

'Would you like to eat with us?' the Captain offered as he was leaving.

'No, no, I am full,' Tarjuman replied.

The Captain twisted the knife in. 'What will you eat, anyway? We don't have any food!'

This comeback left us awestruck, but the Captain wasn't done yet.

'What about the medicines? Our cook has not been well for a while now and I am concerned about him,' he said.

'Don't worry, Captain, God willing, everything will be good very soon,' Tarjuman replied.

After Tarjuman left, we felt a bit restless. We wanted to hear some good news, sooner rather than later. After spending the evening and the following morning all excited, we went to Jafar and asked him for an update. He gave his trademark response and asked us to wait. Days passed and we didn't hear anything comforting. A week later, the monotony kicked in again. In our circumstances, we had no possible reason to sit and contemplate a future, and yet most of us had not given up hope.

One evening, on the bridge, Parjeet was tinkering with the radio and managed to catch a station playing Bollywood songs and providing news from India and Pakistan. The ICC Men's Cricket World Cup 2011, being hosted by India, Sri Lanka and Bangladesh, was also around the corner. This got all of us really excited, and thereafter, every evening, we would listen to this station.

The radio also fuelled banter between the Indians and the Pakistanis among the crew. Now, these two nationalities never need a new reason to banter with each other, but we still ribbed each other on the news coming out of our respective countries, along with cricket updates.

Then, one day, we Indians just won the battle outright when the radio started playing the song '*Sandese aate hain*' from the film *Border*. Some of us just looked at each other and got up, excited, as if it was our national anthem ringing out. With smiles on our faces, we sang along with whatever lyrics we could remember.

In the film, the song features a group of Indian Army men posted at the Pakistan border before the 1971 war, who receive letters from their homes and start singing of their loved ones. We weren't receiving any messages, just some questions we had to answer to prove we were alive, but we could relate to being away from our loved ones.

It was a magical moment when we went from smiling at the beginning of the song to emotional in the middle, especially where the lyrics say '*Ae guzarne waali hawaa bataa, mera itna kaam karegi kya* (O blowing wind, tell me, can you do something for me)?' and Akshaye Khanna's character sings about his mother in the village, '*Meri maa ke pairon ko chhoo ke tu, use uske bete ka naam de* (Touch my mother's feet and tell her her son's name).' Then, at the end of the song, when all the characters come together in a rousing chant of '*Main waapas aaunga* (I will come back)', led by their commanding officer, played by Sunny Deol, all of us felt a current surge through us. *Border* was a great movie in its time, and the song was among the most popular in the late 1990s, so it ended up being played every few days by the radio station. And each time we got goosebumps when we heard it.

But on that night, it led us straight back to our cross-border banter, since the villain in that movie was basically the country of Pakistan. We eventually ended up citing a famous scene from another Sunny Deol blockbuster, *Gadar*, where he rips a handpump out of the ground. Chief Officer Baig and Bada Sahab didn't take any further part in the discussion.

Capt. Ram was looking increasingly better with each passing day. His strength and vigour had returned.

One day, he called all the cadets to the bridge and said he had something very important to discuss—his daughter was finishing twelfth grade. 'You are all "young blood". What field do you think my daughter should pursue a career in?' he asked.

He was very enthusiastic about his daughter's higher education and career, and that instilled hope and optimism in us too. We felt valued that our Captain was asking for our suggestions, so we wanted to give him our best, like in everything we did under his command.

We had our different views and suggestions, ranging from chartered accountancy to medicine. When the Captain asked for my two pennies' worth, my suggestion, too, emerged from my proclivities and interests. I had always been fascinated by the legal profession, so I mentioned a career in maritime law. It would make sense, since the Captain, her father, was already in the shipping industry.

One suggestion was outright funny, and amused the Captain as well. During the initial months of hijacking, we had been watching a Bollywood film named *Welcome* and were impressed with the comic timing of actors like Nana Patekar, Paresh Rawal, Anil Kapoor and Vijay Raaz. So, inspired by the profession of the lead character played by Akshay Kumar, one of the senior cadets suggested a career as an auctioneer. Capt. Ram couldn't believe it was even a real line of work. '*Yeh bhi behen chod profession hai* (Is that really a fucking profession now)?' he wondered. All of us laughed.

More good news came from the bottom of the ship—the amount of seawater seeping into the hatch had reduced considerably, which brought us temporary relief. Plus, we now had more company, since the pirates had captured four more vessels, which were all anchored around us.

It was still winter, and at sunset, we would walk around on the deck. Some of us resumed stretching and doing short workouts. Keeping up the routine and trying to sustain our physical and mental well-being was all we had. Now and then, bouts of optimism and hope would embrace us. Very often, we would also feel despair, anguish and melancholy.

Overall, we believed we were moving towards a resolution to our crisis. But just like the horizon, there was no end in sight.

15

Burial at Sea

February 2011 was also over, and in another month and a bit, we would be 'celebrating' our one-year anniversary as hostages. Senior Cadet David and I would both be turning a year older in April. Last year we had celebrated David's birthday with warm beers en route to Somalia. And I, on 18 April 2010, just a week after our hijacking, had said a small prayer to the gods to give me and my family strength and a long life, and for us to pass this uncertain period and reunite. Never did I think I would be spending two birthdays in captivity.

One evening, I was coming down the stairs from the bridge with these thoughts swirling in my head, right around the time the generator was about to be turned on, so I didn't realize that the crew mess room was depressingly quiet. Usually, around this time, the galley and the crew mess room would be full of noise and chaos, with people running from one corner to another preparing for chores like cooking and cleaning. However, that day, there was no movement at all.

An eerie feeling began engulfing my heart when I saw Abdullah exiting the crew mess room hastily. Without stopping to look, he rushed towards the bridge. Then, adding to my alarm, everyone started shouting for the generator to be turned on immediately. Next, I heard footsteps rushing down from the bridge and approaching the crew mess room. Capt. Ram was still not in the best physical shape, but I could see the extra effort he was making. He was followed closely by the Bosun, Bada Sahab and Ali Baig.

I stood still outside the crew mess room, in the galley, certain that something was awfully wrong. While one part of me couldn't gather the courage to go inside, another wanted to know what was really going on. Finally, I went to the edge of the room and saw that Chief Cook Muhammed was lying atop a table, surrounded on all sides by the crew. My view of him was blocked, but the gravity of the situation wasn't lost on me.

'Cook! Cook!' I heard the Captain say, and then he tried to wake him as if from a deep slumber. I thought Muhammed had possibly collapsed and the Captain was trying to give him CPR. Then, the generator was turned on and the lights flickered to life. The first thing I noticed was that Muhammed's hand was dangling from the table and there was no movement. I felt like something had hit me in the chest—the wind got knocked right out of me.

After several failed attempts to resuscitate him, Capt. Ram finally stood straight, looked at the wall clock and declared, 'Record time of death as 1815 hours.'

It took a minute or two for me and the others to fully absorb what had just happened. We had been dreading it for a long time and our worst fears had now come true. One of us had died. Muhammed, as mentioned before, had not been keeping well for some time, but we had thought he would get better. When Capt. Ram had been in a health crisis, he had triumphed over it, but it had still been a strong blow to all of us. We had barely recovered from that, and now we had lost Muhammed. It was a tragedy, and we simply didn't know how to process any of it.

I couldn't bear to be there any longer and excused myself. I went to Bade, who was on freshwater duty that day, and informed him that our Chief Cook was no more.

'What?' he asked, and immediately went to the crew mess room. He was certainly more courageous than me to have gone all the way to look at Muhammed's body, which was now being wrapped in a white cloth.

A few minutes later, Capt. Ram and Bada Sahab climbed to the bridge, and some others, including me, followed. Everyone was quiet and thinking about what to do next. Ideally, Muhammed's family should have had the opportunity to perform his last rites, but under the circumstances, we didn't know how that was going to be possible. To begin with, the Captain asked Jafar to inform Tarjuman about the incident, so that the news could be relayed to the ship owner and to Muhammed's family.

Meanwhile, we started thinking about how we could get his body home. We could preserve the body in the cold room, but to make that happen, the generator would have to run round the clock, for which we requested extra diesel. But that never happened, as Jafar couldn't get a hold of Tarjuman the whole evening. The latter's mother had also passed away and he was not reachable, or at least that's what Jafar said to us. We looked at each other and knew we would get no help from the pirates.

So we went back to thinking how to proceed. We didn't have the resources to follow the protocols. Preserving the body had to be our priority, but we couldn't do that without outside support. A decision had to be made quickly, or the body would start to decompose.

All the senior officers were on the bridge, along with the Bosun. Capt. Ram was taking everyone's opinions, but everything felt so silent despite the roar of the generator that it was like not a soul was on board. We waited another hour, and when there was still no response from Tarjuman, the Captain decided to go ahead with a burial at sea.

In accordance with the rituals for this, Muhammed's body was bathed, brought to the port side gangway and put on a table. Then, to ensure his body did not lie in the dark, we placed a light source connected to an external battery that lit up the whole patch of the gangway. He was to be left there in peace until the burial the following morning, but Capt. Ram commanded that the body be accompanied by somebody at all times. Then, he thought about it again and said, 'There will always be two people manning the body.' He mandated that somebody from the crew would accompany the cadets in this task, and asked Abdullah to delegate the duties in two-hour shifts. I was paired with Abdul Mbarawa, the oiler.

Being there beside Muhammed's body was an overwhelming experience. My mind was still conflicted, as it had been outside the crew mess room, and the battle was only intensifying. On the one hand, I wanted to be around him, wished to look at him and reminisce the times we had spent together. On the other, seeing him motionless and fully covered with a cloth was far more disturbing than any scene I had come across throughout our ordeal on the ship.

Although only two men were standing guard at any given time, the others were not getting any sleep either. Moreover, because I had been paired with Abdul, the same oiler who had had an anxiety or epilepsy attack on the day Abdi had come to click photographs, I was worried about something like that happening again now. On that day, it was Muhammed who had comforted him and given him company; I didn't know what I would do. Thankfully, Bade came and stood by my side.

We pulled ourselves through the night despite our crashing spirits, and as the first rays of the sun appeared, preparations were made for Muhammed's burial at sea. Capt. Ram reiterated that we were moving forward with it, so we all started gathering on the bridge. At noon, four or five of the crew members carried the body on a plank that Abdullah had fashioned with his own hands. Another crew member was handling the crane. Abdullah hooked the plank to the crane, while two others held on to the opposite end with a rope.

We tried to follow the rules of a burial at sea as closely as possible. First, when the body hits the water, it is very important to minimize the splash; this is done out of respect, so that it doesn't look like the body is being thrown into the water. Second, the body should enter the water in a feet-down position, so weights were tied to Muhammed's feet.

Third, the body was wrapped meticulously to avoid it being attacked by sea predators.

The ultimate goal of a burial at sea is to settle the body down on the seabed as peacefully and calmly as possible. And so, Muhammed was laid to rest with all the respect we could provide. I still have a clear picture in my memory of the entire process and the feelings reflected on everyone's faces as we said our final goodbyes to the man who had fed us for such a long time. All that had happened since the hijacking was forgotten; we could only remember the good times we had spent with our chief cook.

The crew had become our family, so it was like losing a family elder. From that moment on, we were never going to be the same. When the burial ceremony ended, I closed my eyes and asked the Almighty to rest Muhammed's soul in peace.

Death on the ship brought about a considerable change in the pirates' behaviour too. They started keeping their distance from us. There was no communication, nor any monitoring. Now, we roamed freely across the ship, without any interference at all.

Another interesting development was that after Muhammed's passing, we never saw any of the pirates alone; they started huddling together in groups all the time. Perhaps, for the first time since they had taken us captive aboard our own ship, they were scared of us. They realized we had suffered a terrible loss, so it would only be natural for them to be apprehensive of our movements and actions, in case we retaliated and tried to avenge the death in some manner.

For the past few months, we had been doing everything in our power to try and not aggravate them. Finally, the tables had turned, and we reached a stage where our captors didn't want to aggravate us.

Muhammed was laid to rest on the seabed on a Friday. We hoped he would find peace there, even as our ordeal continued on the surface.

16

A Step Closer to Freedom

A couple of days after Muhammed's burial at sea, we finally heard something that should've given us all the happiness in the world, but didn't.

I was standing on the deck with SK when Second Officer Parjeet walked in. He had overheard a conversation between Capt. Ram and Jafar, in which the pirate had said, 'You will go in one or two days!'

This was on 6 March 2011; in another five days, we would complete eleven months in captivity, and in that time, we had heard such statements more times than we could count.

Instead of being hopeful, we maintained stoic indifference. Even if what Jafar had said was true, we figured we had waited for eleven months, what difference would a couple of more days make?

But the following day, we learnt that this time, Jafar's words did have some credibility, after all. We received official word from Capt. Ram that the negotiations for our release had been completed, and that the ransom was scheduled to be airdropped the following day.

At long last, hearing those words directly from the Captain had an unimaginable effect on all of us. We hadn't felt this happy in a long, long time. But later on, when we were reflecting upon the news of our impending release, I couldn't help but think of Muhammed—he was the only one who wouldn't get to experience what all of us had been longing for. It was extremely difficult to reconcile ourselves to the fact that the good news had arrived just a couple of days after his passing. You'll remember, on the hundredth day since the hijacking, it was Muhammed who had woken up before dawn and spotted vehicular movement on the shore, which had turned out to be for the release of the chemical tanker anchored near us. It was sad that when our moment of freedom came, he would not be by our side to experience it.

The next day, 7 March, was our judgement day, so to speak. It was ironic that the day was equally momentous for both sides. We woke up to a lot of movement on and around the ship. The pirates were making preparations, and so was our crew.

There was a constant influx of pirates, who came on multiple boats. Tarjuman, Ahmed and Abdi were also present. In fact, anyone who had spent any time on the ship since the hijacking was there; we saw faces we hadn't seen since the very first day we had dropped anchor. It made sense, because today was their payday, and everybody had come to collect their share.

We were given more than the usual amount of diesel to run the generator, which had been on since early morning. The satellite phone was finally turned on too. All the pirates eagerly waited for the money to be airdropped; all of us gathered on deck to witness the moment that would free us.

We were instructed to stand in three equidistant rows, because the ship's owner had insisted on making a headcount of everyone on board. As for the absence of the late Muhammed Ali, the pirate Ahmed had requested Capt. Ram to convey that he was sick and resting.

A few minutes later, we heard the plane approaching, and I looked up to see it. Unlike the plane that had come for the chemical tanker on our hundredth day, this one was for us and nobody else. The white, twin-engined plane made a couple of circles over the ship, obviously for the headcount, but its very appearance made a plethora of emotions bubble up within me. Most of all, I was excited to see the first sign that our ordeal was coming to an end.

The scene played out just like it had for the chemical tanker. I was seeing it for the second time, but I hope no one else ever has to see it first-hand.

Two boats left from the ship, then one of them threw a smoke float in the water, and moved away from it. This time, I could see everything clearly because the action was centred on us. The plane circled the ship once more, as we waited for it to drop the ransom. Then, the aircraft door opened—it was so close I could see all the details with my naked eye—and a bag attached to a little parachute was dropped towards the sea. The parachute slowed it down so that it drifted around for a while, and dozens of pairs of anxious eyes, including the pirates', followed it as it took its sweet time coming all the way down to the water. That bag contained so much reward for greed, but also so much hope for freedom. I watched its entire downward journey without blinking. Till date, I can't find enough words to describe all my feelings at the sight—the excitement, as well as the worries about what would happen next.

Once the bag touched the water, the second boat rushed towards it, and the pirates finally got what they wanted, even though it was not as much as they had wanted. Our future was not yet clear, but it was beginning to emerge from the mist.

Now our fears and scepticism turned to what would happen once each pirate got his money and left the ship. While anticipating our release, we had not made any plans for how to leave our current position. As mentioned before, we did not have supplies, and the ship was not in a condition to move.

The pirates had promised to give us more fuel, and possibly supplies, before leaving the ship for good. However, we had no reason to believe they would keep their promises. Now that they had their money, they might just abandon us.

We also thought about the fate of the people on board the other hijacked ships around us. Today, they were in the position we had been in on our hundredth day.

Nevertheless, the prevailing sentiment among our crew in that moment was excitement. We had taken one big step closer to home. The aircraft made a few more circles around us until the boats returned to the ship, and then disappeared into the clouds.

Without argument, it was the happiest day of our lives since we had embarked on this voyage in Seychelles eleven months ago. But we were amused to note that it was the pirates who looked happier. We understood that each of them had put in time and effort into hijacking us and keeping us captive, and today, they would finally be getting paid.

The pirates brought up the bag from the boat and rushed towards the ship's office. Capt. Ram gave us strict instructions to not engage or communicate with any pirate, regardless of how good he had been to us in the past. Under no circumstances were we to enquire about the bag.

We were out of our formations and could walk around freely on the deck, but for our own safety, we were forbidden from being around the ship's office.

Parjeet later narrated the story of what he saw from outside the office—it was clumsy and chaotic. The pirates were making too much noise and arguing among themselves. There were many disagreements, and a lot of them seemed unhappy with the share they had finally received. However, I must put a disclaimer here that owing to the natural intonation of their language, we could never really make out if they were being friendly or arguing.

We couldn't help but think about what would happen if they got violent with each other. We didn't want to get caught in their crossfire. Also, we couldn't ignore the fact that the ransom amount was probably far less than they had expected in the beginning, so some of them might harbour resentment and decide to take it out on us violently.

While we were roaming around on the deck, Capt. Ram came down from the bridge and informed us that he was now allowed to speak to the ship's owner, Capt. Aarya. So, all of us immediately got back into seamanship mode and started patrolling the deck for any unnoticed findings.

There wasn't a single clean spot on the ship. Throughout our captivity, the pirates had only allowed us to wash it once, and that had been several months ago. The ship's desolate condition were disagreeable to us all. But we had to wait for the pirates to leave before we could start cleaning.

I was standing on the deck with SK when we saw Hassan, the pirate boat captain who had hijacked us, coming down the stairs. He walked towards us carrying a small pistol.

'Happy? Go back?' he asked.

We responded in affirmation, our eyes locked on the pistol.

'You see?' he asked, pointing at it.

'Sure, no problem!' I responded.

He removed the magazine, and after ensuring that there was no bullet in the chamber, he handed over the pistol to us. We had a quick look and gave it back to him, and he went away. 'Well, at least he looked happy,' I said to SK.

By the afternoon, most of the pirates had deboarded, but not before they did one final sweep to gather whatever they could find. There was nothing left to find, but they still looked desperately for something. The last one to leave was Mohammed, and of all the things we had seen the pirates take with them, he gave us the most bizarre sight.

He was carrying a TV set that had once belonged to Senior Cadet Zaheer, who was surprised to see it still on board. Zaheer had assumed that it had been taken away on the first day we had anchored, when people had just come on board in droves and grabbed our belongings. Apparently,

Mohammed had managed to keep it hidden somewhere on the ship, and when the moment came, he had dug it out to take along. But by the look of it, he was struggling to carry it while climbing off the ship.

Mohammed's idea was to go down the pilot ladder holding the TV in one hand, and I was sure both he and the set were going to end up in the water. Abdullah came and stood next to me as we observed him. Mohammed then got hold of a rope and somehow tied it around the TV, and started lowering it slowly. Suddenly, he screamed, and that was followed by a splash. I wanted to laugh so hard, but somehow controlled myself.

Mohammed turned around and made eye contact with me and Abdullah. I just lifted my hand and waved at him as he climbed down the pilot ladder.

Abdullah then asked us to keep away from the ship's edge, and as soon as the last pirate got off the ship, we were to run back and lock the doors. He was worried that while leaving, they might open fire at us, out of resentment or just for entertainment. By early evening, the whole debacle had ended, and our ship was finally rid of foreign, unsavoury elements.

For the first time in almost eleven months, we were breathing free on the deck of our ship, which we could finally call ours again. No more guns over our heads, no all-pervading fear of death and violence. At last we were free sailors again.

Free, yes, but not safe yet.

17

Uncertainty Lingers

Once the pirates were gone, Capt. Ram asked everyone to assemble on the bridge deck. Our dreams of freedom had been reined in by the reality of the next challenge—leaving Somali waters and reaching a safe area of the sea or the nearest safe port, Mombasa.

I felt the cold evening breeze on my face; the sun had almost set. The Captain was sitting on a chair in the centre, with the rest of us standing in a semicircle around him. Bada Sahab and Mir Balach were standing to the Captain's left and right, respectively.

It should have been a moment of celebration for us, but none of us was in the right mindset for it. We were still stuck in hostile territory and our homes were still as far away. Capt. Ram was in constant touch with Capt. Aarya, and we were sure he was doing everything in his power to help us, but it took a lot of moving parts to execute a rescue operation like we needed.

Until any assistance came, if at all, we were on our own. In the circumstances, the chain of command on the vessel comprised four top heads (Chief Officer, Second officer, Chief Engineer and Second Engineer) reporting to the Captain. After enquiring about the remaining food stock, Capt. Ram asked Chief Officer Baig to check the lashings of the cargo on deck, which would definitely have rusted without maintenance. Ropes were to be prepared, in case tugs were sent to tow our ship.

The pirates, as mentioned, had left the ship filthy; every square inch needed to be cleaned. The Bosun took charge of this and sent us cadets to start with the accommodation area. Additionally, his most important responsibility was to look for any stowaway pirate on board. We certainly did not want to add another woe to our already long list of challenges.

Bada Sahab's image had still not been fixed—everyone remembered his eagerness to assist the pirates—but he was trying his best to improve it by giving his inputs and being supportive by agreeing to ideas and the next course of action. We could clearly see he was finally agreeing with the Captain. Capt. Ram, always a good leader, didn't let his apprehensions about the Chief Engineer become obvious, and gave him full support, continuing to maintain decorum and his integrity. It was only when the Captain asked about the issues in the engine room that we saw guilt on Bada Sahab's face; his discomfort and remorse were palpable.

Capt. Ram then spoke directly to the Second Engineer, Mir Balach, asking about the possibility of moving the ship. 'How much diesel do we have?' he asked.

'Around thirteen tons, sir!' Balach responded. All of us were thrilled to know this, and the fact that the Second

Engineer himself had successfully managed to hide enough of it for so long in our difficult situation. Thirteen tons of diesel on board would not solve all our problems but would at least help us stay afloat and reach safe waters out of Somalia.

Even Bada Sahab seemed astonished at what his subordinate had achieved right under his nose. '*Second sahab, diesel ki baat chal rahi hai* (The conversation is about diesel),' he clarified.

'I know, sir. I am an engineer too!' Balach responded confidently.

The meeting ended with Capt. Ram asking Third Officer Kuldeep to check on the firefighting equipment. Kuldeep finally found his voice since his near-death experience and we could feel he was hopeful now that the pirates had gone. Capt. Ram also asked Bada Sahab to try and run the engine one more time. Perhaps the engine, like us, would find renewed life force now that we were no longer at gunpoint.

We were operating under the belief that external assistance was unlikely. It was a dangerous stretch of the sea, and a rescue ship was also at risk of being hijacked. Our spirits, though, remained high, which became evident when all of us started completing our duties. Even after all these months of hardship, we hadn't lost our will to work tirelessly.

Capt. Ram had asked us to use the satellite phone to call our families and relatives.

I was still unsure if my parents would be in India or Dubai and didn't know on which number to reach them, so I asked Zaheer, my senior cadet, when he was calling his family, to check if they knew or had a contact number for me to call. To my surprise all us cadets' parents were regularly communicating with each other, and Zaheer's father immediately shared a number that was from India.

My father had the habit of handing the phone to my mother every time I called. So, when I finally got through to him, he did the same thing. I couldn't even begin to imagine how overwhelming it was for both of them. My mother could barely speak to me for a minute before her voice became heavy, and she gave the phone back to my father. He tried his best to lighten the mood by asking me mundane questions, showing curiosity about how long my beard had grown and whether I had a shaving kit or not. Later, I got another call, from my uncle (my mother's brother) this time, on the ship's satellite phone. He had been a strong pillar of support for my family throughout the ordeal, and now he seemed as excited as my parents. He asked about my well-being and was happy to hear my confident voice after such a long ordeal. He ended the call by telling me, 'Beta (Son), always stay strong like this.'

One more challenge that worried us was that while one group of pirates had left, we were not sure how many separate groups were active in the area. So Abdullah asked us to stand guard and make rounds of the ship, in case someone made another hijacking attempt. It seemed sensible, but we were not sure what we could really do if somebody came for us again. We were unarmed and would be mere spectators, totally at the mercy of fate.

Just for a sense of comfort, I now held a stick as I patrolled the aft mooring station. But soon, a thought popped into my head—that being around mooring stations was not a good sign. The day we were hijacked, I had been at the fo'c'sle or forward mooring station.

This day turned out to be long and tiring, not only because of all the physical work, but also the overwhelming emotions that were taking hold of all of us. My duties done, I went to bed around 2 a.m. and fell asleep immediately. After many months, I slept peacefully in my cabin, a sign that I was now in a far calmer state of mind.

'Pralav! Pralav! Abandon ship!' a voice rang in my ears, jolting me awake. It was the following morning, and most of us still hadn't acclimatized to the fact that we were not captives any more, so it took some time for me to comprehend.

The voice belonged to Bade, and I was in shock. Seeing my reaction, Bade de-escalated the situation quickly with a smile; he had just been playing a prank, it seemed.

'Fuck you, Bade!' I yelled, while he continued to look at me in bewildered amusement. He realized the prank had not landed well. But what he said next told me it hadn't all been a prank.

'*Haan, yeh jahaaz chhodna padega* (Yes, we'll have to abandon this ship),' Bade said in a soothing voice. '*Uth ja, Captain ne sabko bulaya hai bridge par* (Get up, the Captain has called everyone to the bridge).'

Capt. Ram had also asked us to bring along a bag of any size we could get our hands on.

In a few minutes, every soul on board had gathered on the bridge, and the Captain informed us that the owner was unable to send any direct help. The only ray of hope we could see around us was an Italian warship anchored some distance away. It was monitoring an Italian merchant vessel that had been hijacked and brought to the same location as us a few days ago.

We had been trying to reach the warship, but it hadn't responded. Now it finally did, and assured us of assistance. Clearly, the ship's owner was working behind the scenes in whatever way possible for our rescue. The only catch was that the Italians had refused to send their men to our ship; they had deemed it a risky venture.

The warship command had asked Capt. Ram if we could use our lifeboats to reach it. Capt. Ram refused because of safety concerns, because our lifeboats had not received maintenance or servicing since the hijacking, and we couldn't be sure of their utility.

So we were at yet another impasse. Men from the warship weren't coming to us, and we couldn't go to them.

The warship started constant communication with us on VHF radio. Then it decided to send a helicopter and asked the whole crew to assemble on the bridge deck for a headcount, and to make sure it was just the crew and no pirates on board. Capt. Ram agreed, and shortly, we heard the sound of a chopper approaching, as well as warning gunshots being fired from the other hijacked ships. We all stood at the bridge deck looking at the chopper with desperate eyes and prayers to just take us. It was time.

The only option we had left was to use the life rafts. These might sound similar to lifeboats and might have a similar use, but they are very different in how they operate. A lifeboat has a small engine that helps it run, while a life raft is an inflatable tube that drifts according to the ocean current and wind direction. As soon as the decision was finalized, everybody started accumulating everything they could before they abandoned ship.

We were surprised to see what all the crew had managed to hide and preserve through so many months—cookies, chocolates, bottled water. The officers and cadets, meanwhile, had nothing left. Unfortunately for the crew, the Captain reminded them that when you abandon ship, you cannot carry so much baggage; only a life jacket and important documents.

After much preparation, we finally started disembarking from the ship into the inflated life rafts. There were twenty-three of us in four of them. I was to board the last raft with two more cadets (seniors David and Krishna), Mir Balach, Abdullah and Capt. Ram himself. I was the penultimate man off the ship; Capt. Ram made sure he was the last. Until the last moment on the *RAK Afrikana*, the Captain was devoted to his duty.

Before finally descending to the raft, he went back to the accommodation and screamed as loud as he could, 'Anyone left behind? Is anybody there?'

And with that, the Captain said his final goodbye to the *RAK Afrikana* and descended to the life raft, and sat at one of the front openings, with the Bosun at the other. On the VHF, the Captain confirmed with the Chief Officer, the Second Officer and the Chief Engineer that all were on board their rafts and everything was fine. Once the confirmation was received, the Captain instructed the Bosun, 'Cut the line', and we started drifting away from the ship's side.

The stern was right in our line of sight. Her name, 'RAK AFRIKANA', and IMO number 8200553, were stencilled on the stern in big, bold font, which started getting smaller as we were carried away by the waves and the winds. We were leaving behind 331 days of hopelessness, despair and uncertainty.

We drifted directionlessly for a few minutes, but help from the warship was nowhere in sight, barring a helicopter hovering over our heads, which would be useless in case of any untoward incidents. Capt. Ram started getting worried because we had abandoned ship and got into open waters at their assurance. Rafts were prone to turbulent movement out on the open seas, and I borrowed candies from Abdullah to counter the expected motion sickness. Then the wind changed, and we began drifting towards the shore.

We had flares, which we could use to get the attention of the warship. However, this would also reveal our location to unfriendly elements on the shore. It would be terrible to get into another hijacking scenario when we had barely managed to come out of the last one. There was still no communication from either the helicopter or the warship, so Capt. Ram lit the flare. And even as we feared for our lives, I happened to spot movement in front of the warship. It was twilight, and I thought I saw grey boats. When I informed the Captain, he was worried about whether they were from the warship or more pirates. I assured him I saw them coming from the direction of the warship. But due to the waves and heavy pitching of the life raft, he couldn't see them himself.

To our relief, in a few minutes, a boat with armed soldiers came to each raft, asked for the Captain and then enquired from him how we were all doing. They held their guns ready to engage at any moment while they checked our rafts for anything suspicious. One of the soldiers asked us to remain still.

Then they threw a thick rope at us. 'Hold on to it as tightly as possible!' one of the soldiers said. We were taken aback; we had been under the impression that they would shift us on to their motorboats. Instead, they were towing our life rafts to their warship.

Their motors roared, and we felt a strong jerk from the rope getting pulled with force. It was so strong that if all of us hadn't been holding on tight, we would have surely been left behind. In fact, David, who was already exhausted from seasickness, got hurt when the rope struck the edge of his eye.

As we were towed to safety and the *RAK Afrikana* disappeared from sight, I said something internally to her that I had been formulating subconsciously in my mind.

'You were my first ship. I learnt so much from you, which I hope to implement in life, be it seamanship or survival. You gave me tough days and nights, but you also gave me hope and belief that at the end of the voyage, there is always a safe shore. I left you behind only in a situation where nobody would ever set foot on you, but you always kept me afloat in the toughest times for both me and you. From the first day to the last, you were my steel for survival. Thank you, my lady.'

18

Resilience and Recovery

The motorboats got us to the Italian warship as the light disappeared and the waves picked up. A couple of soldiers were waiting for us at the boarding point, and one of them started pulling us swiftly up by our shoulders and on to the ship.

With that first step on board, the realization dawned on me that I was out of the crisis. We were on a warship, the safest place to be on the open seas.

The soldiers brought us to the upper deck, where they had already made arrangements for our accommodation and food. They had put out foldable single beds and given us disposable boiler suits to wear. As per protocol, they clicked our pictures with our passports.

'Can I smile?' I asked the soldier behind the camera.

'Yes, today is the day to smile!' he responded.

As a precautionary measure, they also checked our vitals. I was running a mild fever and was immediately isolated.

There was also a makeshift bathing space, a corner near the bulkhead on the lower deck covered with curtains. There was a water pipe tied with cables at the top and a small shower head fitted with clips at the end of it. The warm water from the pipe was blissful. I didn't even realize how much time I was taking when one of the soldiers reminded me that the others were waiting in queue. Capt. Ram had gone to meet the commander of the warship. Once the formalities were completed, all of us found our spots and started settling down.

After the showers, we were served meals. The Italian soldiers had set up things so nicely and they were being so accommodating that I got emotional. I still remember the taste of everything I had that night. Since then, I have eaten at many fancy places, but the meal on board the warship was the best one of my life, and I don't think anything can ever top it.

Afterwards, SK and I found a corner of the open deck and lit a cigarette. Soldiers were all around us, and one of them came over out of sheer curiosity, sipping a pint of beer.

'How long were you there? Did you have any food?' he asked, and was shocked to hear us say eleven months.

But that only made him more interested in finding out how we had survived. I, meanwhile, was very interested in what he was having.

'Can I get a beer too?' I asked.

'Wait, let me come back,' he responded, and left in a hurry. He was back in a minute or so, with another pint that he handed over to us. 'Keep it low, it's from my personal quota,' he said.

SK and I started sipping it, and part of me wanted to gulp it down, but I wanted to cherish every sip. Halfway through the pint, in the middle of our conversation, the soldier was called away by a colleague, and upon returning, he politely asked us to return the bottle. 'Sorry, I was not supposed to give you this,' he said, looking sheepish. Apparently, one of his superiors had sent word that it was not safe for us to consume alcohol. We had been away from civilization for a long time and didn't know how our bodies were functioning medically, so alcohol could hamper our health and healing.

I didn't hand it back immediately, though I did so after one more sip. The soldier smiled and left with the bottle.

We learnt that the warship wouldn't leave the spot because it was monitoring the hijacked Italian vessel. Instead, it would transfer us to a Spanish warship it had called in to the area, which would take us to the nearest port. At the end of the first night of freedom, that was the assurance we went to bed with.

The following morning, we noticed a lot of food and other supplies gathered on the deck. We wondered if the stuff was for us, but then again, why would we need it on the Spanish warship? It was then that we got to know about a change of plans—rather than moving to the Spanish warship, we were getting transferred to a chemical tanker which had been released a day after us. This ship's hijacking had lasted only three months, and it was in a condition to sail.

Not all of us were happy with the new plan. I, for one, did not want to leave the warship, and would've stayed if given a choice, primarily because of safety concerns. Moving to another merchant ship had its risks. But, of course, we did not have any say in the matter. In any case, the Spanish warship would be escorting us. So, we disembarked from the warship and boarded the chemical tanker through a couple of boats placed between them. In the meantime, the Italian soldiers had already transferred the supplies to the tanker.

The tanker reminded us of our own ship; it was in a bad condition too. It hadn't been cleaned in months, and there were all kinds of makeshift arrangements. The majority of the crew were from the Philippines, and we didn't have much interaction with them, though we noticed their condition was a bit better than ours because they were released within three months of hijacking.

The Filipinos had also made makeshift sleeping arrangements for their new guests, and our whole crew assembled yet again in an officers' mess room. The irony didn't escape us.

It was a two-and-a-half-day passage to Mombasa. Once we had settled on the tanker, we all started thinking about the same thing: What had happened to our ship? It had been taking in water when we had abandoned it, and we were curious to know whether it remained afloat after that. The chemical tanker had been anchored in the same area, and we asked the crew when they had seen our ship last. All they could say with assurance was that it had not sunk yet; they had seen it afloat, but couldn't tell whether it was listing (tilting to one side).

On the tanker, we were mere passengers. Thus, we relaxed, while the ship's crew continued with their chores and responsibilities. There was nothing much left for us to do but wait to reach Mombasa. We were instructed to cook our own meals and clean the dishes, which we did. That first night was uneventful.

The second night, however, was a different story. Half an hour after midnight, I felt a strong vibration that broke my sleep as well as that of the others. The next thing we knew, the tanker had come to a complete halt—its engine had stopped. It was far from a comforting sign, because we were quite familiar with what could follow. We didn't know how far we were from the location we had left, or from Mombasa. We kept wondering about the status of the Spanish warship escorting us. We started roaming around on the deck, worried, constantly looking over our shoulders for any sign of trouble. We could feel the crew attempting to restart the engine. But with every failed attempt, our anxiety levels climbed.

Thankfully, in twenty minutes or so, which was a long time for our overwrought brains, the crew had a breakthrough; the engine started up again and we continued on our way without any more problems for the remainder of the night.

The following morning, by the time we opened our eyes, we were entering the anchorage at Mombasa port. The moment had arrived.

Quickly, we started grabbing whatever we could of our belongings and assembled on deck. The sheer sense of excitement at seeing other human beings on the jetty was evident from our faces and body language. As the ship turned and the deck became parallel to the berth, the land got closer each second, and we breathlessly awaited the most spectacular moment of our lives.

As we stepped off the chemical tanker on to the soil of Mombasa, we were welcomed by Capt. Aarya and his wife. They greeted each of us with handshakes and handed each of us a bag with a basic necessities kit. Two buses were waiting outside the port to take us to a hotel, which was twenty-five minutes away. The ride, on potholed roads, felt a lot longer, but that was the last thing on my mind. It was surreal to be free and alive, so who cared about the minor inconveniences of life, like potholes?

At the hotel reception, people greeted us as if we had returned triumphant from a war. Maybe we had. What mattered to us was the thrill and excitement of being able to interact with people back in civilization. Struggle and discomfort were a thing of the past; the ship owner had left no stone unturned in ensuring that our stay at the hotel was comfortable.

As soon as the check-in formalities were completed, I rushed upstairs. Each of us was given individual rooms, where we could relax and recuperate. The first thing I did was jump on the bed like a child. I can't even begin to explain how it felt to lie down on a bed with clean sheets. I could've fallen asleep in a minute like a child does when tired after a round of play.

But there was no time to sleep. We had to attend a debriefing in thirty minutes. I took a quick shower and saw that the bag they had given us contained a new T-shirt, but no trousers. So I put on the same pair of denims, which I had kept up on my narrowing waist using a rope in place of a belt.

We assembled in the ballroom for the debriefing with the British firm that had handled the negotiations after Capt. Nair's death, followed by immigration formalities. Once everything was done, we were free to enjoy ourselves. Capt. Ram, sarcastic as always, told us, '*Ab jao, enjoy karo, bas beizzati mat karaana* (Go and have fun, just don't embarrass yourselves or me)!' Capt. Aarya also came to us and requested a controlled celebration, as we had a medical check-up lined up the following morning.

'*Daaru koi nahin piyega* (No one will drink alcohol),' Capt. Ram added. We all agreed and moved out.

We were also given phones to call our families, relatives and friends. I called home and had a long talk with my mother, and she realized that now I was back on land in Kenya, I was out of danger.

In the evening, all the cadets were hanging out in my room. We were ecstatic and wanted to celebrate the occasion. After a long time, all of us were together and there were no guns pointed at our heads, or a feeling that death was around the corner. Ideally, we would've wanted to drink. But that was not feasible, so we just sat reminiscing about the days gone by and discussing our future.

After a while, Parjeet popped his head in and asked, 'What are you all doing? You guys are not celebrating?' We told him what Capt. Ram and Capt. Aarya had asked of us. But he convinced us—if we needed any convincing—that it was too great an occasion to let our spirits be dimmed. We were free men, and that should mean something. Parjeet handed Krishna some cash and asked him to bring a few bottles of beer.

The whole team ended up having a much-needed celebration. The lavish buffet spread for lunch and dinner, and the pool at the hotel were both at our disposal. Not even for a moment did I want to think or talk about the last 331 days. We had finally found freedom and I was basking in it. During our days in captivity, we as individuals, at some point or the other, intentionally or unintentionally, must have done something selfish for survival that would have upset another crew member, but all that was beyond our control under the circumstances we were in. In my opinion, this was not the place to talk about them. It was too soon. But not everyone felt the same way. There was always someone or the other among the cadets who would start talking about the pirates and the whole ordeal every time we were together. In one instance, Krishna started bragging about his bravery to a few women he was talking to at the pool. In front of the owner there was another blame game being addressed. And the remaining crew from Zanzibar, well, they decided only to talk to the owner about their repatriation and pending wages nominating the Bosun as their voice—it was the best and most respectful way in those circumstances.

Later at night, all of us cadets got together again and similar arguments started, but I stepped in and reminded everybody that we had just gone through hell and come out in one piece. And that was because we had stood and fought together. Our differences were nothing compared to what we had triumphed over together. We had lived as a team, and it was imperative to part ways as a team.

I was glad that my words brought back the feeling of camaraderie that had helped us survive. In that moment, I realized how trivial most of our preoccupations in life are. Many things that had bothered me in the past now looked very small. Positivity and optimism were all that filled my mind. I am sure most of us shared the sentiment.

In the morning, Capt. Ram, who was passing by my room, saw the door open and walked in. Some of my fellow cadets had left for their rooms in the middle of the night, others were still sleeping in my room. The Captain could readily imagine the kind of celebration we had had. Technically, we had disobeyed his direct orders, and he did say, '*Ek raat ruk hi jaate* (You could have waited one night)!' But there was no reprimand in his voice; he didn't really mind. His only command thereafter was to be ready at 10 a.m. for the medical check-up.

One by one, we all got ready and started going downstairs to the ballroom.

Towards the end of the day, we started receiving travel details and flight confirmations for our trips back home. Most of the cadets were flying the following day to Mumbai and Delhi.

In the morning, I boarded a flight from Mombasa; then, after a couple of hours' layover in Addis Ababa, Ethiopia, I caught a connecting flight to New Delhi. When I reached the Delhi airport, my parents were waiting for me. I looked at them from afar and wondered if they'd recognize me—over the last year and a half since they had seen me, I had lost a lot of weight, my skin was darker and I was having a tough time keeping my denims from falling off.

But I was wrong; my mother spotted me from a distance, and I could see her telling my father, 'There he is.' I walked up and hugged them; all three of us had tears in our eyes, still coming to terms with what had happened. At the same time, we were thankful that we were together again. My mother asked, 'You have lost so much weight ... *Kya khayega aaj* (What will you eat tonight)?' I just smiled and hugged both of them again.

And this is how eleven months of hardship, struggle, uncertainty and fear of losing everything and everyone ended. It ended well, a year lost but a lifetime learnt.

Epilogue

A few years after the dust had settled, I was at Kakinada Port on the east coast of India, conducting an internal audit on a ship managed by the company I worked for. I was on the bridge as the vessel stood alongside the port. Suddenly, I saw some movement in the channel—two white motorboats speeding across the waterway.

For a split second, the sight took me back to the days of the hijacking—a memory that had been lying dormant was suddenly awakened.

I had goosebumps, and a chill ran down my body. I was far away in time and place, but my subconscious mind took me back to 2010–11. I could feel my heartbeat rise for a second. It was not a pleasant memory.

Upon my return from Somalia, I learnt that the true essence of life is the people we love and who love us. So, first, I went to Pilani, Rajasthan. When I had called my parents from Mombasa, I had expressed my desire to return to the place that was home to some of my most beautiful childhood memories, which always represented peace and tranquillity to me. There was no better place for me to start the journey of my new life.

Now, in the present day, the hijacking is more than a decade behind me. The numbing episode brought significant changes in me and my outlook towards life. The version of me that had boarded the *RAK Afrikana* in September 2009 was very different from the version that returned in March 2011 after spending 331 days off the coast of Somalia. When I boarded the ship, I was a young, carefree boy. Within a few months of my return, I had transformed into a responsible man and a dutiful son. Since then, my family has been the most important thing in my life.

Weeks after our release, I had started contemplating whether to go back to sea ever again. I was not afraid of being on a voyage—but my desire and need to stay close to my family was greater. I had experienced what it meant to be away from them, and the experience taught me their significance in my life. The hijacking and the ensuing psychological turmoil had shaken my parents to the core, so to always be close to them, I decided not to sail again.

Finding an alternative career was going to be difficult, as I had trained to be a sailor and was still at the junior-most level in the industry. Non-sailing jobs would be hard to come by, but I was prepared. Upon my return, without wasting much time, I completed by bachelor's degree. I had already lost eleven months and, in my mind, didn't want Canada to repeat again. I knew the shipping industry was vast, and I was sure I could find opportunities within it. And I did. I also knew that once I got the opportunity, it would be my commitment and hard work to climb up the ladder. The last decade has been good for me, professionally and personally. I have reached a stage of contentment.

The one thing I find disagreeable is when others look at the hijacking from a place of sympathy. Considering myself a victim never sat well with me. Even in the public sphere, where sympathy is the most expendable sentiment, I made conscious efforts to change the narrative.

Upon my return in 2011, I was speaking at a conference on maritime laws at the Gujarat National Law University. By the time I stepped up to deliver my talk, the speakers before me and the audience had grown accustomed to addressing the seafarers who had experienced piracy as 'victims'. So, I began by calling ourselves 'survivors', not victims. That is how I looked at myself, and that is how I wanted everybody else to look at me. At the end of the event, I was glad that everyone's perspective had changed.

Our hijacking had caught the imagination of the masses. Everywhere I went and everyone I talked to always had questions about how we survived and what impact the hijacking had on our psyche. I was asked a lot about my trauma, to which I always replied that it depended on the kind of memories one wanted to carry with them. In fact, I had started joking about it even before we had abandoned ship. But after returning home, I never disclosed the intense moments to my parents. Dinner-table discussions about it at home were mostly about narrating the events in a humorous manner.

You would expect me to harbour negative sentiments towards the whole episode and the players in it. But I believe whatever happened in the past is supposed to remain there. I learnt from it and moved forward.

However, to be completely honest, for a while, I did feel some disappointment towards some of my shipmates. I questioned certain actions they had taken. But with time, even those negative feelings dissipated. I realized all of us were trying to survive in any way we could.

I have never even felt any resentment towards the pirates who held us captive. They kept us at gunpoint, sure, but they were never violent towards us except when they had orders from higher up the ladder. I can't help but think that the pirates were poverty-stricken people who had been manipulated into entering a world of crime. They had hoped and believed it was to their benefit. Evidently, they were not benefiting from it. Nobody knew where the millions of dollars worth of ransom went. The fate of their land and their families remains unaltered.

The dates of our hijacking and release hold the utmost significance in my life. They represent survival and triumph, rather than struggle and despair. I wanted to commemorate the dates, so I got them tattooed on my arm, along with the *RAK Afrikana's* IMO number. Unlike us, the ship didn't survive the ordeal, and eventually went to rest on the seabed, three miles off the coast of Somalia, right where we had abandoned it.

The dates are always with me, a constant reminder that hope is the most crucial thing an individual can hold on to. They tell me that if I could survive those 331 days, I can survive anything that life throws at me in the future.

I am certain that the entire crew reminisces about its days in captivity. Over the years, I have lost touch with all of them, except Bade. However, the shipping industry, it is said, is very small, and our paths are bound to cross some day or the other. So far, I have only come across Akbar Khan, our Batti Sahab, once in Dubai, and met Bade a couple of times. Abdullah the Bosun is one individual whose personality left a great impact on me, and I would love to meet and have a long talk with him, if and when I get an opportunity to visit his home in Zanzibar.

But one man I won't get to meet again is our Captain, Rameshwar Naithani. A few days after I returned home, over dinner, my father told me he had received an email from Capt. Aarya that Capt. Ram had had another stroke at his home in Delhi. He didn't make it a second time. The news of his demise broke my heart, and I couldn't sleep for a few days.

I can't stop thinking that perhaps Capt. Ram was our guardian angel on the ship, whose purpose was to ensure our safe return, which he fulfilled with all his might. Perhaps that's why he survived the first stroke on board; once we were all safe and sound at our homes, his soul departed his body.

Writing this book was always on my mind, but it took me time to find the words to fit the story. It was a journey that twenty-four people embarked on, before their hands were forced. It is a story of how we kept our sanity and character intact through a nerve-wracking crisis; how people from distinct national and cultural backgrounds came together and helped each other. It is also the story of how one individual, Capt. Ram, became a beacon of hope for the entire crew. Till his last step off the ship, his thoughts and efforts were directed at our welfare, care and safety.

I am glad that I came out of the crisis unscathed, and I want to reiterate my good fortune in coming back to my family, the people who love me and waited for me. My return was a happy occasion for me precisely because it mattered to all those people. My days in captivity made me realize the importance of family, which we tend to ignore amid the nitty-gritty of modern life. Our work, goals, dreams and ambitions take us away from that one foundation stone that is the essence of our being.

As the last words of my story, I want to throw this thought into the depths of the universe, that the bond of family is to be preserved and cherished. We are nothing without the people who love us. As I noted in the Introduction, if your family is with you, the book of prayers and good wishes is open for you.

Acknowledgements

To my strong-willed wife, whom I began dating after my return from the hijacking and got married to six years ago. You are undoubtedly the wiser of us when it comes to life's choices and decisions.

To my beloved uncles, aunts and cousins. I am grateful for your constant support and the immense care you have shown my parents during the most challenging eleven months of their lives. Your kindness and dedication mean more to me than words can ever express, and I will be eternally grateful to you.

To my near and dear ones, who, upon my release, came not to offer sympathy but to recognize my courage.

To my colleagues, who have shown respect for my resilience and strength.

To the owner of *RAK Afrikana*. Thank you, you did everything in your power to help get us out.

Last but certainly not the least, to my wild friends. Thank you for never forgetting me during my disappearance, for plotting a drunken rescue mission and, most importantly, for never actually going through with it—unlike all our boys' trip plans!

My sincere thanks to the team at HarperCollins Publishers India for believing in me as a first-time author and for their incredible patience and unwavering support in bringing this book to life.

Finally, a thank you to all the readers who will embark on this voyage of memories.

About the Author

Pralav Dhyani comes from a humble middle-class family with deep roots in Lansdowne, Uttarakhand. The first in this family to pursue a career in maritime shipping, Pralav now has nearly fifteen years of diverse industry experience.

After his experience on the *RAK Afrikana*, his reflections on maritime piracy have been featured on various respected platforms over the years. In 2011, he published a paper on maritime piracy with the Gujarat National Law University, followed by articles for UNODC India in 2012, the Mariners Action Group in 2013 and Scroll.in in 2017. His story was the subject of a short film by Vice Asia and a TEDx talk at Jai Hind College, Mumbai, both in 2023.

Pralav now lives in Dubai with his family, where he runs his own company, named after his mother. He enjoys camping, playing cricket and spending time with his golden retriever.

HarperCollins *Publishers* India

At HarperCollins India, we believe in telling the best stories and finding the widest readership for our books in every format possible. We started publishing in 1992; a great deal has changed since then, but what has remained constant is the passion with which our authors write their books, the love with which readers receive them, and the sheer joy and excitement that we as publishers feel in being a part of the publishing process.

Over the years, we've had the pleasure of publishing some of the finest writing from the subcontinent and around the world, including several award-winning titles and some of the biggest bestsellers in India's publishing history. But nothing has meant more to us than the fact that millions of people have read the books we published, and that somewhere, a book of ours might have made a difference.

As we look to the future, we go back to that one word— a word which has been a driving force for us all these years.

Read.